Shabbos under Pressure

"When you don't have a lot of time to cook, use your **Electric Pressure Cooker** for Pressure Free Cooking!"

♡ Sharon

DISTRIBUTED BY FELDHEIM

Distributed by: Feldheim Publishers / POB 43163 / Jerusalem, Israel
208 Airport Executive Park / Nanuet, NY 10954

THE RIGHTS OF THE COPYRIGHT HOLDER WILL BE STRICTLY ENFORCED.

Photography and Recipes by Sharon Matten
Design and layout by Yocheved Brecher

www.feldheim.com

Printed in the United States of America

This book is dedicated to my parents
Tuvia ben Nachum (z"l) and **Yenta bas Shmuel Nechemia (z"l)**
who dedicated their lives to the ideals found in Pirkei Avos 1:2
"עַל שְׁלשָׁה דְבָרִים הָעוֹלָם עוֹמֵד, עַל הַתּוֹרָה וְעַל הָעֲבוֹדָה וְעַל גְּמִילוּת חֲסָדִים"
"The world stands on three things, the Torah, Service
and acts of Loving Kindness"

May their memory be for a blessing

Why YOU need Shabbos Under Pressure

When you're looking for a quick, real life, brand independent, fun and time saving way to prepare pressure free Shabbos meals, **Shabbos Under Pressure** is your answer. It is for the novice home cook and the more experienced "Balebusta" (homemaker). The recipes are traditional and not so traditional, are always straightforward with time saving ideas, personal stories and anecdotes. Each recipe is paired with beautifully photographed examples of completed dishes.

Jewish mothers have been using pressure cookers since the dawn of time, with many exploding catastrophes. The fear of disaster has certainly kept me from using a traditional pressure cooker.

The current generation of home chefs wants to feed their families but endeavors to add modern twists, making traditional recipes more contemporary and faster to prepare. The safer Electric Pressure Cooker removes the fear of calamity and has given us a fabulous new way to cook! **Shabbos Under Pressure** is a traditional Jewish cookbook with a fresh and current feel.

The recipes and tips in **Shabbos Under Pressure** work for *every* brand of Electric Pressure Cooker. Whether you have an Instant Pot, a Crock Pot Express Cooker, a Cuisinart or any other brand of Electric Pressure Cooker, **Shabbos Under Pressure** works for any model. In **Shabbos Under Pressure**, nearly all the recipes are adapted for "manual mode". In the case of exceptions, descriptions are added to explain the work around for models that do not have that specific mode.

Are you gluten intolerant? I am a GFE (Gluten Free Eater) too! While **Shabbos Under Pressure** is not specifically a gluten free cookbook, nearly every recipe in the book has a method for making it gluten free. The exceptions are Challah and Fruity Noodle Kugel.

Don't worry about only making these recipes for Shabbos. While **Shabbos Under Pressure** may be "Shabbos Specific" the recipes can be made during the week as well. Trust me when I tell you that leftovers (if there are any) will be inhaled by your family!

Every recipe in **Shabbos Under Pressure** has been tested and retested and tested again. I also try to make sure that the preparation of recipes is as stress and pressure free as possible. *That's* the whole point of **Shabbos Under Pressure**. Cooking under pressure = pressure free cooking!

TABLE OF CONTENTS

ACKNOWLEDGMENTS

1 Thank you G-d, for giving me the strength, patience and wisdom to complete this book. I believe that G-d gives us everything; our health, our wealth, our abilities. It is our responsibility to use those gifts and to maximize their potential. I also believe that the only thing that we completely earn ourselves is our good name. Everything we do in life helps us to merit that good name. Thank you G-d, for the gifts that you have given me, and may I warrant the health and strength to continue to work towards my good name.

2 This book is dedicated to my parents, Tuvia ben Nachum (z"l) and Yenta bas Shmuel Nechemia (z"l). My parents are responsible for who I am today. They taught me about character, charity, and the importance of a good name – earned by good deeds. They also taught me a lot about cooking. My father was a "six sigma" cook. Precise. Exacting. Conscientious. He was the guy that would measure the squares for kreplach to make sure that they were all the correct size before cooking. It wasn't that he was compulsive exactly, it was that he wanted them to all cook properly and be the best that they could be for his family. My father passed away seven years ago, and I can still feel him in my home shnukering rice from my pot and commenting on how good (or not good) it was. He would stay after minyan at shul and make eggs for all the guys who stayed after davening. When the shul needed food for a kiddush, or congregants were making a simcha, you could find him in the kitchen making egg salad, kugels or chicken. You would never know he was an executive at a major corporation, he was down to earth and kibbitzed and fed all that came to the shul. He would have considered an Electric Pressure Cooker a new toy and been extremely excited about using it. He would have loved the mechanics of it and would have loved "playing with it" to see if he could improve the recipes he made.

My mother (z"l) was alive for the writing of this book. We often discussed recipes, and she was my favorite taste tester. A "Super Outstanding" from her was worth more than gold. I write so much about her in this book. One of the hardest things I've ever had to do was to change the tenses in all those references. She passed away on the last night of Passover this year. I am crushed. My mother taught me so much about cooking. Not just about the process but about the soul of cooking. From my mother, I learned how my grandmother cooked and the special recipes handed down from generations. My mother was here at our house every Shabbos, commenting on all the dishes she tasted. She was a dessert lover and would lick the plate with a finger if the dessert was really good. I ran the changes by her that I made to the family recipes to get her approval and permission to publish them. The originals were my mother's – I don't share those; they are for family only. The modified recipes are not exact, but close to the originals. Just before Passover this year, my mother who was unable to cook or even stand, asked if she could help me prepare. That was my mother. Even in a declined state, she wanted to help. I knew she had a new, old fashioned (terrifying) pressure cooker, still in the box in the basement. I asked if I could have it to use for my Passover prep. By giving it to me, she would be helping me prepare. She wholeheartedly agreed and was super excited to be able to do anything to contribute to the Passover preparations. I ended up carefully using the old-fashioned pressure cooker to cook for the holiday, and to compare how it worked in contrast to an Electric Pressure Cooker. Mom was delighted to help any way she could. It was the last contribution she made.

I hope that when you read this book you get a sense of who my parents were. I think they would have been proud of what I have written. I miss them with all my heart. This book is dedicated to them.

3 Thank you, **Perrin Davis**. You were my first editor and you taught me what it means to write a cookbook. Your guidance and experience helped me to begin writing what now looks like a cookbook!

4 Thank you, **Brent Reams**. It was you that started my journey into the Electric Pressure Cooker world. You sent me my first 6-quart Crock Pot Express Multi Cooker, and as they say, the rest is history. I look forward to working with you in the future. Thanks for your support.

5 Thank you, **Gavriel Sanders**. Your faith in this project, and me, continues to amaze me. Your wisdom, advice, prodding, and encouragement fueled me to push through many of the challenges I faced. I truly appreciate all that you have done.

6 Thank you, **Eli Meir Hollander, Feldheim Publishers**. I hugely appreciate your taking a chance on this previously unpublished author. You worked very hard to make this book happen. I am thankful for all your efforts to publish Shabbos Under Pressure. Have a good Shabbos!

7 Thank you, **Norene Gilletz**, for being an inspiration, a mentor, and a friend. You have given me valuable guidance throughout this project, even while facing your own challenges and writing your own book. Thanks so much for writing the foreword for this book and setting the tone for the rest of what follows. I wish you only good health and success in your future endeavors.

8 Thank you, **Paula Shoyer**, for your advice, reassurance, encouragement and support. Thank you for being a good "foodie" friend throughout this process.

9 Thank you **Yocheved Brecher**, for doing such an incredibly beautiful job on the layout of Shabbos Under Pressure!!! Your experience and talent shine through on every page of this book. Thank you for all the hours you spent and for all your hard work.

10 Thank you, **Trina Kaye**, for being an awesome publicist and friend. Or as you put it years ago "A sister by another mother." I'm looking forward to working with you going forward. Can you say, "It's going to be so much fun!!!"

11 Thank you, **Margo Strahlberg**, for your help in writing this book. Your advice on using Electric Pressure Cookers, enthusiasm, uplifting midnight "make me smile" texts, recipe testing and comments were fabulously helpful. I love that you hassled me, and put up with my constant texting "did you read it yet?" Thank you for your contributions to this book and for being such a good friend.

12 Thank you, **Anne Galster, Beryl Mann** and **Miriam Solo Greenfield**, for being my cheerleaders and such incredibly good friends. It's such a comfort to know that there are people who really care about you and only want the best for you. Your encouragement and positive vibes at every turn were like, as my Mother (z"l) would say "A salve on a wound". May we only share simchas together.

continued on page 8

ACKNOWLEDGMENTS *continued*

13 Thank you, **Sharyn G**, our favorite Q. You are family by choice. Thank you for your help and support through the entire writing of Shabbos Under Pressure. Every week you would taste test, make constructive comments and suggestions. You are nearly as excited about this book as I am. Your enthusiasm is contagious. Especially when life was incredibly difficult, your positive energy, passion and compassion were so appreciated. You are a master editor, and I can't tell you how much your hours of final editing mean to me. **Sharyn Goldrich** (with a Y), thank you for being part of our family and such a major contributor to Shabbos Under Pressure.

14 Thank you to my **dear children** for all of your encouragement and patience. Thank you for putting up with all the experimental meals, my often-complete distraction, and my discouraged moments during this whole process. Thanks for testing the recipes, making them in the EPCs without any guidance to see if they would work for the "novice" chef. Thank you for supporting me during my hardest moments this year. We all suffered Bubbie's loss. Thank you for cheering for me on our family's WhatsApp group every step of the way, and for being such wonderful kids. Thank you to my dearest daughters-in-law, who are now my dear daughters, for your suggestions, recipes, testing, tasting, patience, and most of all for how much you love my boys. I really really love you all and am incredibly proud of each one of you. I look forward to the day when I really don't have any pressure getting ready for Shabbos!!! Maybe it will be when we eat Shabbos meals at your homes!!!

15 To my **Dearest Husband**… I can't begin to describe how much I love and appreciate you. You are truly my better half; without you I wouldn't be whole. You have been so completely unquestioningly supportive of me throughout all my crazy schemes and through all my endeavors. You have stood beside me through good and not so good, holding me up when I couldn't seem to do it myself. Through every step of writing Shabbos Under Pressure you have shown so much wisdom in your comments and advice. You have been a positive contributor/supporter/advisor/editor/tester/idea bouncer/critic and advocate. You wouldn't let anything stand in the way of achieving the goal of publishing this book. No matter what, I know you always have my best interest at heart. You are the football player to my cheerleader, the Avraham to my Sarah, my absolute best friend and the love of my life. I thank G-d everyday that you are mine.

16 Finally, I apologize if there is someone I overlooked in my acknowledgements. Please know that each one of my friends and family are appreciated and loved. Thank you for all your support and encouragement.

Shabbos under Pressure

Since the dawn of time, Jewish women have endeavored to feed their families. For example, Eve fed Adam the forbidden fruit (although that didn't turn out too well). The need to feed has always been there.

> "Why did the Jewish Bubbie stuff the chicken? Because she had already stuffed her whole family at the Shabbos table!"

Shabbos comes all preparations cease, the Shabbos candles are lit, and the chaos that ensued just moments ago suddenly becomes the calm after the storm. Peace envelops the Shabbos home.

Biblical Matriarchs and Patriarchs seemingly have always had to rush to prepare meals for family, friends and unexpected guests. When the three Angels visited Abraham and Sarah, Abraham instructed Sarah to "Hurry…and bake some bread!" Then Abraham ran to select a calf and gave it to a servant who hurried to prepare it.

We all know about the origins of matzoh…no time to let the bread rise? Let's make super quick matzoh!!! The Jewish people were really really in a hurry to leave Egypt! As much as things change, they stay the same.

Today, Jewish families are still in a hurry. Even with modern technological wonders, there still doesn't seem to be enough time to prepare meals. Especially meals for Shabbos, when Traditional Jewish families sit down to enjoy the specially prepared meals with (lots of) family and (lots of) friends.

Why the rush to get ready for Shabbos? No matter what happens, no matter where you are on planet Earth, Shabbos starts at sundown. It's a hard-set deadline. When

With that being said, the Electric Pressure Cooker is a godsend. When we come home late on Friday and need to prepare huge Friday night and Saturday Shabbos meals, anything that makes cooking easier and faster is a must-have. Until now, preparing "Traditionally Jewish" foods might take hours of preparation and cook time. The Electric Pressure Cooker changes all that. Suddenly Bubbies' Chicken Soup and Matzoh Balls takes under an hour instead of 2 days (yes…before Rosh Hashanah I let my Chicken Soup simmer for two days to achieve its ultimate chickeny rich goodness). Stuffed cabbage for the family in under an hour?!!! It's unheard of. Impossible! Nope. Not anymore.

My Father (Of Blessed Memory) had a favorite phrase: "Make haste slowly". To what could that phrase better refer than an Electric Pressure/Slow Cooker being used to prepare for Shabbos? Nothing! Say goodbye to a Shabbos Under Pressure and hello to a "Pressure Free Shabbos". I guarantee the "Shabbos Under Pressure" cookbook will take the pressure off you and help you eat Happily Ever After…pressure free.

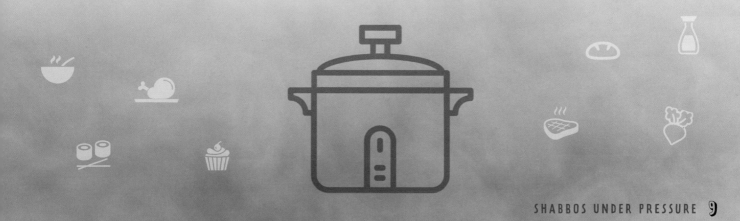

FOREWORD BY
NORENE GILLETZ

Sharon Matten's inspiring new cookbook, Shabbos Under Pressure, will be a huge help in getting both me and you over feeling intimidated. Her recipes and guidelines are written in a simple, straightforward way. Sharon Matten transforms ordinary ingredients into fabulous fare for Shabbos and beyond.

I bought my Electric Pressure Cooker about a year ago and it took me at least a month just to get it out of the box. I was busy working on a new book, The Brain-Boosting Diet, so I just didn't have the time to master yet another new appliance. Each time I decided to make something in my Electric Pressure Cooker, I had to refer to the instruction manual to check how to turn it on! Usually, I would call my friends and ask, "How long should I cook it? Which setting?" Like most people, I cook on auto-pilot, which usually means cooking dinner in my oven, putting everything together in one pan.

Gradually, I've learned how to cook up some tasty meals in my Electric Pressure Cooker, some successfully, others not quite as successful. My chicken soup always turns out and my sweet and sour meatballs are scrumptious. Applesauce was easy to master, but my unstuffed cabbage with 'what-were-supposed-to-be-mini-meatballs' somehow morphed into cabbage soup because I overcooked it!

It's time to take your Electric Pressure Cooker out of the box and start cooking!

Norene

The "real" me

I love to cook. It's a good thing, because I cook a lot. As an observant Jewish individual, I cook way more than most people do, because every Shabbos means pouring my heart and soul into cooking mountains of food for various crowds.

Our house has a revolving door policy so at any given time, there may be any given number of people (usually teenagers and young adults), coming and going from our house… and I wouldn't have it any other way! Nothing is more awesome than gathering people from far and near, old friends and new faces, the one thing that most people can agree they all love: food.

The biggest issue that I, along with many others, often face is the lack of time. There never seems to be enough of it! I find myself wanting to cook, bake, roast, broil and concoct all the food that I normally do but wishing it could be done in a fraction of the time. Even with a great kitchen, there is only so much you can prepare in a limited amount of time.

If I could save time in a bottle… The first thing that I'd like to do, is to make a roast that doesn't take an eternity to cook. Then I can spend time with you.

The reality is, in this day and age, everyone is busy. Whether working, caring for family, kickboxing, or cleaning guinea pigs' cages - we all have other things to do besides sit by the stove and watch our chickens roasting or cakes bake.

Most of my friends, who are way smarter than I am, became hooked on Electric Pressure Cookers as soon as they came out. Some of them swear by them so much that they even have two! It took me a while to become part of the "I can cook faster than the average superhero" culture, but once I did, I was obsessed.

I remember the days when I would come home from work two hours before Shabbos and hadn't cooked a single thing. Not. A. Single. Thing. I'm fast, but not superhero fast. I don't even have a cape.

Shabbos meals in our house (depending upon who and how many people are coming) can consist of any or all of the following: Challah bread, appetizer, soup, meat, chicken, vegetables (many), salads, side dishes (potatoes, rice, quinoa) and dessert. That's a lot of food. That's a lot of pressure. That kind of pressure = stress. Stress = unhappy family. Unhappy family = unhappy me. And nobody wants that.

I set out to discover and create recipes and menus that could be made super-fast using my Electric Pressure Cooker. I needed to cut the amount of time it took to prepare for Shabbos. I need to have sanity in my life and not stress. It's a tall order for mere mortals, but not for pressure cooker superheroes.

This is the kind of pressure we love. Cooking pressure = less time to cook = less time to prepare for Shabbos = less stress = happy family = happy me. Shabbos Under Pressure takes on a whole new meaning.

All I need now is a cape.

💬 TERMS USED IN THIS BOOK

Electric Pressure Cooker (EPC): This book is intended to be used with any brand or variety of Electric Pressure Cooker. For that reason, I will be using EPC to refer to your specific pressure cooker – regardless of size or brand.

EPC pot (referring to the EPC's insert bowl): This is the bowl that comes with your EPC. It is inserted into the actual electric appliance and will contain the contents of the recipes.

Lid Lock: In the olden days, pressure cookers were scary and terrifying (at least to me). If you didn't use the pressure cooker correctly it could explode and possibly take out an eye. While my Mother and Grandmother had one, I never did. I was too chicken. With the safety features of the new EPCs I finally feel safe using a pressure cooker. Part of what makes the new electric variety so safe is the Lid Lock. The EPC will not start pressurizing until the lid is completely locked. On most EPCs there is a clear method of locking the lid. I refer to that in this book as "Lock the Lid." There is also a clear method to unlock the lid, once the pressure has been sufficiently released (hooray for safety!). I refer to that in this book as "Unlock the Lid."

Pressure Release: One of the things that makes the new EPCs way safer than the old pressure cookers is that there is a mechanism that ensures that you cannot unlock the lid of the pressure cooker until the pressure has been released. This is key. There is no chance of your pressure cooker exploding all over your kitchen. It's a plus.

Pressure Release Valve: At the top of every EPC is a Pressure Release Valve. This is similar on every EPC in that there is a "locked" position and an "unlocked" position. Before starting any pressure-cooking cycle, the pressure release valve must must must be set to the "locked" position. If you do not have the valve in the "locked" position, the EPC will not be able to create the pressure needed to actually "pressure cook". I'll remind you in every recipe to lock the pressure release valve. Don't worry.

Manual Pressure Release: While pressure cooking, a lot of pressure is built up in the EPC. What makes the EPC safer than my Grandmother's pressure cooker is the new safety feature that the EPCs have. They will not unlock until the pressure has been released. You release the pressure. Manual Pressure Release means that you carefully turn the pressure release valve to the "unlocked" position. Pressure, and steam, will be released from the EPC so it is important to stay clear of the pressure release valve while manually releasing the pressure.

Natural Pressure Release: The other way to release the pressure from the EPC is to allow the pressure to "Naturally Release". If you don't manually release the pressure when the cooking cycle is complete, the pressure will slowly release on its own. This is called "Natural Pressure Release". Some recipes will instruct you to allow "Natural Pressure Release" for a specific amount of time, then "Manually Release the Pressure". This means that you let the EPC release the pressure on its own for the instructed amount of time, then you "Manually Release the Pressure" by turning the Pressure Release Valve to the unlocked setting. At that time, any remaining pressure will be released from the EPC.

Cooking Modes: Because there are so many types of EPCs on the market, each with different pressure cooking modes, I only use a few cooking modes described below.

Sauté/Brown: The sauté/brown mode will allow you to sauté or brown food in the EPC, without locking the lid or cooking with pressure. Some EPCs may have the ability to adjust the temperature in sauté/brown mode. My assumption is that, if adjustable, the temperature is set to high.

Slow Cook: The Slow Cook mode allows the EPC to theoretically act like a traditional slow cooker, cooking over a long period of time using low heat, without using pressure. The EPCs that I've tested differ from traditional slow cookers. EPCs, generally, heat only from the bottom of the EPC pot in Slow Cook mode, whereas a traditional

> Hi! This is me! I'll be giving you helpful tips throughout the book and warning you about details to which you need to pay special attention. Make sure to note the highlighted areas – they help you plan ahead and prevent you from making mistakes. Just remember – You'll feel no pressure when using an Electric Pressure Cooker!

slow cooker's heat completely surrounds the inserted slow cooker pot. In the recipes that require the Slow Cook Mode, I take into account the difference in cooking methodology. No pressure here!

Rice: The Rice mode is designed to perfectly cook rice. If you don't have a rice mode on your EPC simply cook the rice on manual mode with high pressure for one third of the time specified on the rice package cooking instructions. You can also check the manual that comes with your EPC for specific rice cooking instructions.

Yogurt: I use this mode for allowing the challah dough to rise. If you don't have a Yogurt mode, don't worry. I give an alternate mode in the recipe directions.

Warm: You can have the EPC warm after it is done cooking or use the Warm mode as directed for specific recipes.

Manual Mode: The function buttons on each brand of EPC may vary. To ensure that recipes are prepared in a consistent way regardless of brand, I use the Manual mode for most recipes. Please keep in mind that each EPC may have slight variations in cooking temperatures and cooking pressure. You may need to adjust your cooking time accordingly.

Added Water: Electric Pressure Cookers require liquid to build steam and pressure. Most EPC's require around a cup of water on the bottom of the EPC pot for this purpose. This water is **in addition to** the water included in the recipe itself. At the end of the ingredients list in most of the recipes I include "ADDED WATER". This is the water that is needed for the EPC to build pressure, not specifically for the recipe. I pull it out of the recipe ingredients for this specific reason.

MORE TERMS USED IN THIS BOOK

Food Terms

The recipes in this book are designated by the Kosher definitions of either Meat or Pareve. No Dairy was harmed in the creation of this book.

Meat: The "Meat" designation implies that the recipe contains ingredients containing beef or poultry. Fish is not included under the "Meat" heading.

Pareve: The "Pareve" designation implies that the recipe has no "Meat" ingredients or "Dairy" ingredients. It is "gender free". Fish is included under the "Pareve" heading.

Gluten Free*: Most recipes in this book are Gluten Free. I use "Gluten Free*" (note the *) to indicate that the recipe is not specifically Gluten Free but can easily be adapted to be Gluten Free. In some cases, for example, a good quality 1-to-1 gluten free flour blend can be substituted, or Gluten Free Panko/Breadcrumbs can be used instead of the glutenous variety.

The yellow highlights in this book

Ingredients Highlighted in Yellow: I've always had an issue with cookbooks and recipes that contain elusive ingredients. When you go to fix the recipe last minute, you aren't always prepared with the proper ingredients on hand. I take special care to highlight the unusual ingredients in yellow. I will also try to give suggestions for similar alternative ingredients whenever possible. Please keep in mind that there is a reason the original ingredient was specified. It will help the recipe taste better! Alternatives will still be good. I promise.

Instructions Highlighted in Yellow: I have been guilty of the crime of reading a recipe too quickly and missing a key step or note, ultimately having the resulting dish not be quite as good as it could be. It's true.

To help avoid similar catastrophes, I highlight important or specifically critical directions in yellow. Pay attention to those. There's a reason they are highlighted in yellow.

Hi again! See this yellow comment? When you see ingredients or instructions that are this color in the book it means CAUTION! Pay special attention to those ingredients or directions.

JEWISH TERMS USED IN THIS BOOK

a"h – Alav Hashalom and z"l – Zichrono Livracha: These are basically Jewish terms for "Of Blessed Memory."

Balebusta: A (Jewish) homemaker.

Bnei Akiva: A Jewish Religious Zionist Organization.

Cholent: Cholent is basically a bean, barley/rice, potato, meat stew that cooks overnight in an EPC or slow cooker. It is traditionally eaten hot at Shabbos lunch.

Hakafos: It is a custom to dance around with the Torah Scrolls on Simchas Torah. Hakafos are 7 "circles" danced around the synagogue.

Kiddush: A blessing over wine that takes place after prayer services or before a Sabbath/Holiday meal. In the synagogue a "Kiddush" does have someone saying the kiddush prayer, but it is also a social gathering and a place to shmuz after the service.

Lishkah: Literally means office, however it is the central office/location for Bnei Akiva.

Mamaleh: An endearing way of saying darling or sweetheart.

Minyan: Literally a quorum of 10 men needed for a prayer service. In this book it represents a general name for a prayer service of men and women.

Non Gebroks: We don't eat "leavened bread" on Passover, we eat Matzoh. There is a custom that some Jewish People have to eat Non-Gebroks (completely wheat free) because of the fear that even a small amount of wheat coming in contact with a liquid might make it chametz (leavened bread). It's great for the GFEs (Gluten Free Eaters) who eat that way all year long.

Oneg: A social gathering after a night meal on Shabbos or Holiday.

Passover/Pesach: This is the holiday that commemorates G-d's redeeming the Jewish People from slavery and taking them out of Egypt.

Patchke: A big, messy, time consuming task/job.

Purim: On Purim the Wicked Haman (boo!) of Persia planned to draw lots (purim) to determine the day to destroy all of the Jewish People. Beautiful Jewish Queen Esther (along with her Uncle Mordechai) saved the day by going to King Achashveirosh and ratting out Haman. We celebrate because we dodged a bullet and it all ended joyously.

Rebbetzin: The Rabbi's wife.

Rosh Hashanah: The Jewish New Year. This holiday is two days long.

Seudas Shelishis/3rd Meal: This is the afternoon meal on Shabbos. It usually consists of salads, light foods and some sort of bread/bagel/rolls.

Shabbos: Shabbos a.k.a. Shabbat a.k.a. Sabbath a.k.a. Sundown on Friday night until an hour after Sundown on Saturday. On Shabbos all work stops. Just like G-d rested after creating the whole world for six days, we also rest after our six days of work. It's #4 of the Ten Commandments.

Shul: Synagogue.

Simchas Beis Hashoeivah: Is a special celebration held by Jews during the Intermediate days of Sukkos*.

Simchas Torah: The day after Sukkos. Every week a "parsha"/section of the Torah (Hebrew Bible) is read until the entire Torah has been completed. It takes exactly one year to complete the entire Torah reading and Simchas Torah is a joyous holiday that celebrates that completion and the "restart" of the Torah reading from the beginning (Bereishis)…" In the beginning…"

Sukkos: This holiday is seven days long and commemorates the Sukkos (temporary housing) that the Jews used while wandering in the desert for forty years.

Yom Kippur: The Jewish Day of atonement

Yom Tov: Any Jewish Holiday that is not Shabbos. Unlike Shabbos, cooking and carrying outside are allowed.

*https://en.wikipedia.org/wiki/Simchat_Beit_HaShoeivah

Note the gorgeous bold red ribbon at the top left hand corner of each page.

Pareve
· · · · · · · ·
Medium
· · · · · · · ·
GLUTEN FREE*

This line tells you the gender of the recipe, Meat or Pareve. You are always prepared to have the right type of recipe for your meal.

This line tells you the recipe's level of difficulty. One spoon means easy. A novice chef could make it. Two spoons means medium level of difficulty. You know your way around an EPC. Three spoons means this is a difficult recipe. An experienced chef, or someone who likes a challenge, could make this recipe.

This line indicates whether a recipe can be modified to be gluten free by using gluten free ingredients. While most recipes can be made gluten free, check the ribbon before starting.

DEPRESSURIZE

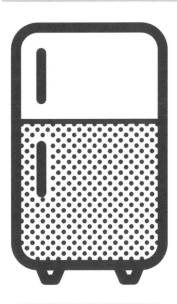

Make some of the key ingredients that are used in Shabbos recipes in advance!

The EPC is a fabulous tool to help make your Shabbos and Holiday prep less stressful. Another great way to make your pre-Shabbos preparations less pressureful is to "depressurize." Make some of the key ingredients that are used in Shabbos recipes in advance!

Stock
Stock is one of those ingredients that is great to make in advance. Store it in the freezer for whenever you need it!

Freeze Your Cabbage
You can freeze your cabbage in advance for stuffed cabbage. You can even roll the cabbages in advance and store them in the freezer for a cold, short Shabbos!

Onions & Leeks
You can wash and chop leeks and onions in advance and freeze them. Make sure to label the packages with the quantity. I like to double bag/wrap sharp ingredients like onions and leeks.

Racks for the bottom of the Pot
(Silicone Or Metal)

Racks with handles*
(Silicone Or Metal)

TOOLS AND ACCESSORIES

Whenever cooking anything it's essential to have correct tools that make preparation go smoothly. Here are some of the EPC tools I think will be helpful as you start out on your EPC journey. The recommendations below are just that... recommendations. After you've used, and have a feel for how your EPC works, do a little in store or online shopping to find what speaks to you. All of the items below (as of the writing of this book) can be found on Amazon. Brands and further description can be found at the end of this book on (Page 146).

* If you don't have a rack insert with handles you can easily make handles with a piece of heavy-duty aluminum foil. Simply cut a foot-long piece of foil, then fold it over four times to make a three-inch-wide long piece of foil. You can tuck that foil under a rack or pan in your EPC, and when your food is done cooking, lift the rack/pan out by the ends of the foil. Easy peasy.

Steamer Baskets
(Silicone Or Metal)

Egg Cookers
(Silicone Or Metal)

Cholent/Yapchik Pot

Non-Stick Pot and See Through Lid

7-inch Round Cake Pan
(3 or 4 inches high)

Mini Silicone Pot Holders

Magnetic Cheat Sheet

Additional Silicone Cooking Tools

Steam Vent Diverter

CHALLAH

SERVES
6–8

Modes: Yogurt/Warm | Manual High Pressure   **Pressure Release:** Manual Release

Challah, a braided loaf of bread, is synonymous with Shabbos. Every Shabbos cookbook must have a Challah recipe! Why? Jewish Symbolism. For one, the double challah that are eaten at each Shabbos/Holiday meal commemorate the double portion of Manna (a.k.a. miraculous loaves of food the Jews ate in the desert) that the Jewish People received before Shabbos/Holidays. Additionally, the blessings that we make on the Challah envelop our Shabbos table in holiness. This recipe makes baking Shabbos Challah super simple and helps to eliminate your pre-Shabbos pressure.

INGREDIENTS:

ADDITIONAL MATERIALS NEEDED

- 1 7-inch x 3-inch round pan or two smaller (loaf) pans
- 1 tight-fitting pan lid or aluminum foil to cover pan(s)
  Food safe plastic wrap
  Nonstick vegetable spray

Challah Dough

- ½ cup warm water
- 1¼ teaspoons yeast
- 2 cups "packed" bread flour
- ½ teaspoon salt
- 1 large egg room temperature
- ¼ cup canola oil
- ¼ cup granulated sugar

Egg Wash

- ½ cup water
- 1 egg whisked with 1 teaspoon water for egg wash
  Challah toppings of your choice

ADDED WATER

- 1 cup

If you have a little more time, let the Challah dough rise in the EPC and bake in a conventional oven for 20–25 minutes.

Challah Dough

1 Preheat oven to 350°F.

2 Spray a 7-inch x 3-inch round pan or 2 smaller oblong/rectangle pans with nonstick vegetable spray.

3 Combine the **Challah Dough** ingredients into a large bowl. Knead until smooth.

4 Braid the dough then place the challah dough into the prepared pan(s). Cover loosely with food safe plastic wrap.

5 Add the cup of ADDED WATER into the EPC pot.

6 Place the pan(s) of challah onto an EPC rack. It's helpful to have a rack with handles or ready-made aluminum foil handles (page 16) to lower the pan(s)/trivet. Lower the rack/challah into the EPC pot.

7 Set the EPC to Yogurt mode. If you don't have a Yogurt setting set the EPC to Warm mode. Lock the lid. Cook for 30 minutes, letting the dough rise in the pan.

8 Unlock the lid, remove the plastic from the challah then cover the challahs with the pan lid or foil.

9 Set the EPC to manual high pressure mode. Cook for 25 minutes, then manually release the pressure.

10 Carefully remove the challah from the EPC and uncover. Do not get any water on the uncovered challah.

Egg Wash

11 Whisk together the **Egg Wash** ingredients, then brush the egg wash over the challah. Top with challah toppings of your choice.

12 Place in the oven and bake for 10 minutes.

13 Cut the fragrant Challah at your Shabbos meal.

המוציא לחם מן הארץ

appetizers

SUSHI WITH SMOKED SALMON

SERVES
6-8

Modes: Rice | Manual High Pressure **Pressure Release:** Natural Release | Manual Release

As a food writer I have tons of fun going to different food related shows and conferences throughout the year. I spend a lot of time talking to each vendor about their new cool and innovative products. This past year I came across bamboo rice. Its green color was really different. I couldn't wait to make green sushi for the amusement of my guests. It was a hit when I served it, and Bamboo Sushi with Smoked Salmon was born.

INGREDIENTS:

For the Rice

2 cups bamboo rice

1⅓ cups cold water

¼ cup rice vinegar

¼ cup granulated sugar or stevia

1 tablespoon sesame seeds, white or black

For the Spicy Mayonnaise Spread

½ cup mayonnaise

¼ teaspoon cayenne pepper

For Assembly

6 square rice paper sheets

1 (10-ounce) bag shredded carrots, or 2 large carrots julienned

1 large hothouse/English cucumber, julienned

1 large or 2 small avocados, peeled and thinly sliced

4 ounces smoked salmon

Spicy Mayonnaise Spread (see page 144)

Additional white or black sesame seeds for garnishing

- Bamboo rice can be found in the natural section of your local grocery store. It can also be found online on Amazon.com. If you don't have bamboo rice you can substitute any short grain/sushi rice.

- You can substitute round rice paper for square if necessary.

For the Rice

1 Thoroughly rinse the rice until the water runs clear. Drain completely.

2 Place the rice in the EPC pot. Add the 1⅓ cups cold water. Stir to combine.

3 Lock the lid and close the pressure valve.

4 Set the EPC to rice mode and cook for 12 minutes. See note regarding rice cooking mode on page 13 if you don't have a rice setting on your EPC.

5 Naturally release the pressure for 10 minutes, then manually release the pressure.

6 Add the rice vinegar, granulated sugar and sesame seeds to the rice. Set aside.

For the Spread

In a small bowl combine the mayonnaise and cayenne pepper. Set aside.

For Assembly

1 Cover a sushi rolling mat completely with plastic wrap.

2 Evenly spread/pat around ½ cup of rice into a square directly on the mat. You can use a spatula to spread the rice, or if you are wearing gloves slightly wet them and pat the rice into the square shape.

3 Top the rice with a rice paper square. Evenly spread around a tablespoon of Spicy Mayonnaise Spread on top of the rice paper.

4 On the edge of the roll closest to you place a layer of carrots, cucumber, avocado, then smoked salmon. The filling should be around 3-inches wide/deep and go all the way to the edges of the rice paper horizontally. Carefully roll the sushi, tightening the sushi as you roll.

5 Cover the roll with plastic wrap, sealing the ends. Refrigerate for at least 30 minutes before cutting into portions and serving.

Pareve
·········
·········

Easy
·········

GLUTEN FREE*

GEFILTE FISH LOAVES

SERVES
12-16

Modes: Sauté/Brown | Low Pressure   **Pressure Release:** Natural Release | Manual Release

What is fantastically easy to make but takes forever to cook? The ubiquitous Gefilte Fish Loaf! Using the EPC cuts the cooking time to a fraction of the time compared to the traditional method. The results are outstandingly delicious. What could be better than that???

INGREDIENTS:

- 2 one-pound loaves of frozen Gefilte Fish. Do not remove the parchment wrapping.
- 1 pound baby carrots or 1 pound peeled and sliced large carrots
- 1 teaspoon granulated sugar
- ½ teaspoon freshly ground black pepper
- ½ teaspoon salt
- Lettuce for garnish

ADDED WATER

- 2 cups

1 Place a rack in the bottom of the EPC pot. Pour the 2 cups ADDED WATER into the EPC pot.

2 Place the wrapped fish and carrots on top of the rack, then sprinkle the granulated sugar, freshly ground black pepper and salt on the fish. Lock lid and close pressure valve.

3 Cook 20 minutes using manual high pressure mode. Naturally release the pressure for 10 minutes, then manually release the pressure.

4 Chill the fish for at least 2 hours. Cut each loaf into 8 pieces and serve garnished with lettuce and cooked carrots.

- Make sure to remove only the plastic wrapping from the loaves leaving the parchment covered fish.
- To make this recipe gluten free use gluten free fish loaves.

Pareve

Easy

GLUTEN FREE*

TANGY GEFILTE FISH LOAVES

SERVES 12-16

Modes: Manual High Pressure   **Pressure Release:** Natural Release | Manual Release

I was looking for a way to upgrade the traditional gefilte fish loaves. Dear Daughter-In-Law saw my internal struggle and came to my rescue with her favorite recipe for gefilte fish loaves. The result? Tangy Gefilte Fish and love for all.

INGREDIENTS:

2   one-pound loaves of frozen gefilte fish. All the wrapping removed. DO NOT DEFROST.

1   pound baby carrots or 1 pound peeled and sliced large carrots

12 ounces cocktail sauce

Lettuce leaves for garnish

ADDED WATER

1   cup

1   Pour the 1 cup ADDED WATER into the EPC pot.

2   Place the carrots in the water, then place the fish on the carrots. Top the fish with the cocktail sauce.

3   Lock the lid and close the pressure valve. Cook for 20 minutes using manual high pressure mode.

4   Naturally release the pressure for 10 minutes then manually release the pressure.

5   Chill the fish for at least 2 hours. Cut each loaf into 8 pieces and serve garnished with lettuce and carrots.

Hey! Look Mom! No parchment on this fish!!

- **Do Not Defrost** the fish or you will have fish mush instead of beautiful fish slices.
- To make this recipe gluten free use gluten free fish loaves and cocktail sauce.
- Make sure to remove ALL the wrapping from the loaves leaving only the fish.

Pareve

Medium

GLUTEN FREE*

HONEY LEMON TERIYAKI SALMON WITH BOK CHOY

SERVES 4-8

Modes: Sauté/Brown | Manual Low Pressure **Pressure Release:** Manual Release

Many years ago, friends came to visit us in here in hometown Chicago. At the time Mr. Friend (Shimmy) was on the Atkins diet. "What can you eat?" I asked. He replied, "Don't bother…it's just way too complicated". I heard "Are you up for a challenge?" and replied, "Challenge Accepted!". I researched the diet online and found a recipe for Salmon with Bok Choy on the Atkins website. We all were kind of amazed at how good the recipe turned out. This is a variation of that recipe, updated for the EPC and dedicated to Mr. Friend Shimmy!

INGREDIENTS:

For the Salmon and Bok Choy

Nonstick vegetable spray

3 tablespoons toasted sesame oil

4 skinless salmon fillets

4 heads baby bok choy, leaves separated, washed and dried

2 tablespoons teriyaki sauce

For the Sauce

2 tablespoons teriyaki sauce

2 tablespoons honey

1 tablespoon toasted sesame oil

1 tablespoon low sodium soy sauce

For Serving

1–2 fresh lemons, thinly sliced, for garnish

ADDED WATER

¾ cup

For the Salmon and Bok Choy

1 Set the EPC to sauté/brown mode. When the EPC pot is heated, generously spray with nonstick spray. Add the toasted sesame oil.

2 Stir fry the bok choy for 1-2 minutes until soft. Remove from the EPC pot and place on a platter.

3 Place the fillets in the oil and brown for 3-4 minutes on each side. Remove the fillets from the EPC pot and place on a platter.

4 Place the ¾ cup ADDED WATER in the EPC pot. Scrape the bottom of the EPC pot with a heat resistant spatula to remove any bits stuck to the bottom of the pot. Set a rack into the pot, add the browned salmon fillets, then top with 2 tablespoons teriyaki sauce.

5 Lock the lid and close the pressure valve. Cook for 5 minutes using manual low pressure mode, then manually release the pressure.

6 Transfer the salmon to a pan or platter. Do not clean the EPC pot.

For the Sauce

1 Set the EPC to sauté/brown mode.

2 Add the sauce ingredients to the EPC pot. Sauté for 7 to 9 minutes until the sauce boils down and thickens slightly, stirring constantly and scraping the bottom of the pot to remove any stuck-on pieces.

3 You can keep the sauce warm by setting the EPC mode to "warm".

For Serving

Serve individual pieces of salmon on appetizer plates on a bed of bok choy topped with warm sauce. Garnish with lemon slices.

You can use the bottoms of the bok choy to garnish your dish. When you cut off the bok choy leaves, the base looks like flowers!

Meat
Medium
GLUTEN FREE*

MY FATHER-IN-LAW SAYS "THESE ARE THE BEST STUFFED CABBAGE EVER"

SERVES 6-8

Modes: Manual High Pressure **Pressure Release:** Natural Release | Manual Release

The dish my family requests the most on the Jewish Holiday of Sukkos is Stuffed Cabbage, or "Holishkas" as my Bubbie (z"l) used to call them. My Bubbie used to cook the cabbage, wrap it around the meat filling, secure each stuffed cabbage with a toothpick, and then cook them in a large pot of sauce. They were delicious – but a huge patchke (that means a big, messy, time consuming job). Much to the dismay of my family, I used to only make stuffed cabbage once a year.

Did I mention it's a patchke? Using the EPC takes away the hours of cooking time. Additionally, freezing or EPCing the cabbage makes the leaves super soft and easy to roll, significantly reducing the patchke element of the preparation. You could even make them every week…except the other appetizers might get jealous, and we wouldn't want that to happen, now would we?!!

INGREDIENTS:

For the Cabbage

To Prepare the Cabbage Leaves:

1 large head of cabbage, frozen for at least 5 days in advance then defrosted before using. Carefully separate the leaves from the cabbage. You can also follow the directions below for cooking cabbage in the EPC if you do not freeze the cabbage in advance.

For the Cabbage Rolls

1½ pounds ground beef

1 small onion, finely diced (around 1 cup)

1 clove garlic, finely minced

1 cup uncooked long grain white rice

Toothpicks for sealing the cabbages

ADDED WATER

1 cup (if cooking the cabbage leaves in the EPC)

For the Sauce

1 (15-ounce) can tomato sauce

1 (15-ounce) can crushed tomatoes

1 small onion, finely diced (approximately 1 cup)

¾ cup raisins

½ cup apricot preserves or duck sauce

½ cup brown sugar

1 teaspoon freshly squeezed lemon juice

Make sure to have lots of challah available for dipping in any remaining sauce on the plates!

For the Cabbage

*To Prepare/Cook the Cabbage Leaves (If **not** using the freezing method):*

1 If you are not using the freezing method of preparing the cabbage, add the 1 cup ADDED WATER and a rack to the EPC pot. Place the whole cabbage on the rack. Lock the lid and close the pressure valve. Cook using manual high pressure mode for 6 minutes, then manually release the pressure.

2 Cool the cabbage (you can run it under cold water), then separate the leaves.

For the Cabbage Rolls

3 Place a trivet on the bottom of an empty EPC pot. In a large bowl mix the ground beef, onion, garlic and rice. Place 2 to 4 tablespoons of beef filling on a cabbage leaf. Roll according to the pictures below.

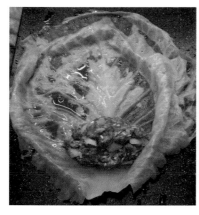  

4 Secure the bottom of the roll with a toothpick. Place the cabbage carefully on the trivet in the EPC pot.

5 Repeat with the remaining cabbage leaves and filling, stacking the stuffed cabbage rolls in the EPC pot.

For the Sauce

1 In a large bowl, thoroughly combine the sauce ingredients. Pour over the cabbages.

2 Lock the lid and close the pressure valve.

3 Cook for 30 minutes using manual high pressure mode. Naturally release the pressure for at least 30 minutes, then manually release the pressure.

4 Take the cabbages from the EPC pot, and carefully remove the toothpicks from each cabbage.

5 Serve the stuffed cabbage rolls hot, covered with sauce.

- Do not place more than 6 large or 8 small cabbage rolls in the 6-quart EPC! Really!

- You can roll the cabbages in advance and freeze them raw in a single layer. When you are ready to cook them, prepare the sauce and continue according to recipe directions.

- Reserve the leftover cabbage for Stuffed Cabbage Soup (see page 48) or Vegetable Stock (see page 43).

STICK TO YOUR RIBLETS

SERVES
6-8

Modes: Manual High Pressure   **Pressure Release:** Natural Release | Manual Release

When I was in college, here in wonderful Chicago, many of my good friends were in school in New York. This meant I visited New York every vacation. When I arrived at the airport, my dear friend, Ruthy, would pick me up and we'd drive directly to my favorite rib place – Shmulke Bernstein's on the Lower East Side. I am a HUGE rib fan, and at the time, Bernstein's made the best ribs. Ever. We always went to Bernstein's for ribs every time I came in. After college, life continued. Ruthy and I attended each other's weddings and had families, but we've managed to remain super close friends despite the distance. Over the years our lives have changed, but the one thing that hasn't is my complete love for BBQ ribs. This recipe is Sharon & Ruthy worthy.

INGREDIENTS:

Nonstick vegetable spray

4 pounds beef riblets (I've also used lamb riblets)

2 cups barbecue sauce (or more if desired), divided

½ cup beef stock (you can also use chicken or vegetable stock)

Cool Ranch Spread (see page 144), for serving

Additional BBQ sauce, for serving

1 Line a large baking sheet with foil. Spray with non-stick vegetable spray. Set aside

2 Set aside 1 cup barbecue sauce.

3 Place a trivet/rack in the EPC pot. Add the ½ cup beef stock.

4 Place the ribs on the rack. Top with the remaining 1 cup sauce.

5 Lock the lid and close the pressure valve. Cook using manual high pressure mode for 60 minutes. Naturally release the pressure for 10 minutes, then manually release the pressure.

6 Remove the ribs from the EPC pot and place them on the prepared baking sheet. Pour the pan sauce over the ribs.

7 Pour the reserved cup of sauce from step 2 over the ribs.

8 For super delicious caramelized, crispy ribs, broil the ribs in the oven for 7 minutes on each side using medium heat.

9 Serve with Cool Ranch Spread or additional BBQ sauce.

- To make this recipe Gluten Free use Gluten Free BBQ sauce.

- You don't have to broil the ribs after EPCing, but they are WAY better if you do!

SUPER FLUFFY MEATBALLS

SERVES 6-8

<u>**Modes:**</u> Manual High Pressure <u>**Pressure Release:**</u> Natural Release | Manual Release

The first time I made meatballs in my EPC, they resembled super solid golf balls. You know, like those pretty red ones you use when playing miniature golf. The meatballs were tasty, but not cookbook recipe worthy. So…back to the drawing board and recipe research. I determined that the best way to make kicking meatballs is to have a "moist maker" filling, broil them, then cook them in sauce in the EPC. The result? Seriously awesomely fluffy meatballs and not a mini golf windmill in sight!

INGREDIENTS:

Nonstick vegetable spray

2 pounds ground beef, close to room temperature

1–2 large whole eggs

¾ cup almond or soy milk

1 cup panko crumbs (can be gluten free)

1 tablespoon onion powder

1½ teaspoons garlic powder

½ teaspoon salt

¼ teaspoon freshly ground black pepper

1 cup chicken or vegetable stock

1 (26-ounce) jar marinara sauce

3 cups cooked rice or pasta

1 Cover a large baking sheet with foil. Spray with nonstick spray.

2 Preheat oven broiler to medium heat.

3 In a large bowl, gently combine the beef, one egg, almond /soy milk, panko, onion powder, garlic powder, salt, and freshly ground black pepper. If the meat mixture seems especially dry add an additional egg.

4 Carefully form 1 ½ inch meatballs and place them on the prepared baking sheet. Repeat until all the meat mixture is used.

5 Place the baking sheet on the middle rack of the oven and broil the meatballs using medium heat for 5 minutes. Rotate to the non-browned side, then broil and additional 3-5 minutes until the second side is browned.

6 Add the stock and marinara sauce to the EPC pot.

7 Carefully place the meatballs in the marinara sauce, covering completely with sauce.

8 Lock the lid and close the pressure valve.

9 Cook the meatballs using manual high pressure mode for 7 minutes, then manually release the pressure.

10 Serve the hot Super Fluffy Meatballs over prepared rice or pasta.

Using pre-made sauce allows you to make this recipe many ways. You can use traditional marinara or a mushroom, spicy, or veggie loaded variety.

SUPER SIMPLE TERIYAKI, BUFFALO OR BBQ WINGS

SERVES 4-8

Modes: Manual High Pressure   **Pressure Release:** Natural Release | Manual Release

Wings are essentially effortless to make and incredibly popular – no matter which variety you choose! There's something to be said for picking up a saucy, sticky, packed-with-flavor wing, and nibbling off all the tender chicken. It's SO fun!!! I always separate the wings into two pieces. It makes them easier to eat.

INGREDIENTS:

Nonstick vegetable spray

For the Sauce

½ cup teriyaki sauce

2 tablespoons canola oil

Or

½ cup barbecue sauce

2 tablespoons canola oil

Or

½ cup Franks Red Hot Sauce

2 tablespoons canola oil

Or

1 cup Sweet Baby Ray's Buffalo Wing Sauce

For the Wings

4 pounds chicken wings, trimmed of fat, separated and tips discarded.

ADDED WATER

½ cup water

For Serving

Cool Ranch Spread (see page 144)

More sauce, as desired

---

1 Line a large baking sheet with foil. Spray with non-stick vegetable spray. Set aside

For the Sauce

2 Place the teriyaki, barbecue or hot sauce in a small bowl. Whisk in the canola oil. Set aside.

For the Wings

3 Place a trivet/rack in the EPC pot, then add the ½ cup ADDED WATER.

4 Place the wings on the rack.

5 Lock the lid and close the pressure valve. Cook using manual high pressure mode for 10 minutes. Naturally release the pressure for 10 minutes, then manually release the pressure.

6 Remove the wings from the EPC pot and place them on the prepared baking sheet. Pour the sauce over the wings.

7 For super delicious caramelized, crispy wings, broil the wings for 7 minutes on each side using medium heat.

For Serving

8 Serve with Cool Ranch Spread (page 144) or additional BBQ, teriyaki or hot sauce.

- Here's another opportunity for creativity. Do you have a favorite chicken sauce? You can use it on these wings too. Follow the directions until it's time to cover the wings with sauce, then use your favorite.

- You can save the chicken liquid that's collected on the bottom of the EPC pot from the cooked wings. It makes a perfect base for any soup that uses chicken broth.

Meat
....
Easy
....
GLUTEN
FREE*

SWEET AND SOUR CHICKEN WINGS

SERVES
6-8

Modes: Sauté/Brown | Manual High Pressure   **Pressure Release:** Natural Release | Manual Release

Every Simchas Torah there was incredibly energetic dancing in the Bnei Akiva Minyan on the second floor of the Lishkah (Bnei Akiva building). You could actually feel the floor vibrating from the dancing! The young men and women all danced with a lot of enthusiasm (on separate sides of the mechitzah!), and we were seriously afraid that the entire second floor would collapse! After the hakafos dancing there was always an organized oneg at a nearby house where the teenagers would gather in a safe but fun environment – often at my house. We'd empty out the basement to make space for the crowd. The foods of choice were Spaghetti with Meat and Sweet & Sour Chicken Wings. We made a lot of food for the huge volume of people. It was always all gone by the time everyone left!

INGREDIENTS:

Nonstick vegetable spray

2 tablespoons canola oil

1 cup finely diced white onion

3 cloves crushed garlic, or 3 frozen cubes

15 ounces tomato sauce

20 ounces sweet and sour sauce (duck sauce)

½ teaspoon white pepper

4 pounds chicken wings, cleaned

crusty bread, for serving

ADDED WATER

½ cup

1 Cover a large baking sheet with foil and spray with nonstick spray. Set aside.

2 Set the EPC to sauté/brown mode and heat the canola oil in the EPC pot.

3 Add the onion and garlic, then sauté until soft.

4 In a medium bowl whisk together the tomato sauce, sweet and sour sauce and white pepper. Stir in the sautéed onion and garlic. Set aside.

5 Place a rack to the bottom of the EPC pot. Pour in the ½ cup ADDED WATER. Using a heat resistant spatula, scrape any stuck-on onion or garlic pieces off the bottom of the EPC pot. Place a rack on the bottom of the EPC pot.

6 Add the chicken wings, then cover with the blended sauce.

7 Lock the lid and close the pressure valve. Set the EPC to manual high pressure mode and cook for 15 minutes, then manually release the pressure.

8 Transfer the wings to the prepared baking sheet. Pour the sauce from the EPC pot over the wings.

9 Broil using medium heat for 7 minutes on each side until the sauce is thicker and the wings are slightly browned.

10 Serve hot with crusty bread and lots of napkins!

It's ok if you don't want to fire up your oven's broiler to brown the wings. After removing the wings from the EPC pot, remove the rack, set the EPC to sauté/brown mode and cook the sauce until thickened. Stir constantly, scraping the bottom of the EPC pot with a heat resistant spatula. Pour the thickened sauce over the wings.

Stock – Vegetable, Chicken, Beef

Chicken Leek Soup

Porcini Mushroom "Barley" Soup

Smokey Red Lentil Soup

Stuffed Cabbage Beef Soup

Traditional Chicken Soup

Vegetabley Vegetable Soup

Dried Fruit Soup

soup

STOCK

is one of the simplest ingredients

to make in the EPC. Whereas you might have your stock simmer for hours and hours and hours and hours, in the EPC you can have fantastic, flavorful stock in around one hour. That's pretty incredible. You can store the finished stock in airtight deli containers in the freezer for later use. **My friend Miriam** says you can also freeze some of your stock in ice cube trays, then in airtight freezer bags, for smaller flavor bursts in your cooking. **My friend Mira** told me about cheese cloth bags. She highly recommends them and started using them after her Dear Husband nearly choked on a bone from his chicken soup!!! I've since started using them and really recommend them. They make cleanup and straining pressure free!

STOCK – VEGETABLE, CHICKEN, OR BEEF

INGREDIENTS:

For Chicken Stock

4 quarts water

2 pounds chicken bones

For Beef Stock

4 quarts water

2 pounds beef bones

For Vegetable Stock

4 quarts water

3 large carrots, peeled and cut into 3-inch pieces

3 celery ribs, cut into 3-inch pieces

1 large parsnip, peeled and diced into ½ inch pieces

1 large turnip, peeled and diced into ½ inch pieces

1 large sweet potato, peeled and diced into ½ inch pieces

1 large sweet onion (like Vidalia), unpeeled and cut into quarters

2 teaspoons dried dill or 2 tablespoons chopped fresh dill

2 teaspoons dried parsley or 2 tablespoons chopped fresh parsley

1 Place the water into the EPC pot.

2 Place the stock bones or vegetables into a mesh bag. You can use more than one bag if necessary. Secure by tying a knot at the top, then place into the water. If not using a mesh bag, place all the Stock ingredients into the EPC pot.

3 Lock the lid and close the pressure valve. Cook for 60 minutes using manual high pressure mode. Naturally release the pressure for 45 minutes, then manually release the pressure.

4 Remove the mesh bag from the stock. Strain the stock if desired.

Don't worry if you can't find mesh bags at your local grocer. Prepare the stock as directed then strain it through a sieve before serving/storing.

PORCINI MUSHROOM "BARLEY" SOUP

SERVES
6–8

Modes: Sauté/Brown | Low Pressure **Pressure Release:** Natural Release | Manual Release

On a blustery, wintery Friday night, nothing is better than a steaming bowl of Porcini Mushroom "Barley" Soup. As a GFE (Gluten Free Eater), barley is not on my list of menu items – so I substitute healthy short grain brown rice in this recipe. Personally, I love this soup with the rice, but if you are a staunch barley supporter you can use barley instead of the short grain brown rice. This soup is one of my mushroom loving family's favorites, I'm sure yours will love it too!

INGREDIENTS:

32 ounces Vegetable Stock (page 42)

1 cups water

1 cup short grain brown rice

1 tablespoon porcini mushroom powder or ½ ounce dried porcini mushrooms ground to a powder

2 teaspoons porcini mushroom salt or 2 teaspoons sea salt

2 tablespoons canola oil

Additional salt to taste

½–1 teaspoon freshly ground black pepper, to taste

1 pound white button or cremini mushrooms thickly sliced into ¼ inch slices

4 large carrots cut into 2" pieces (1 pound)

3 green onions, thinly sliced (around ¾ cup)

Croutons or crackers, for serving

1 Place the stock, water and rice into the EPC pot. Stir to combine.

2 Add the remaining ingredients into the EPC pot.

3 Lock the lid and close the pressure valve. Cook on manual high pressure mode for 30 minutes

4 Naturally release the pressure for 20 minutes, then manually release the pressure.

5 Unlock the lid and serve this hearty soup hot with croutons or crackers.

- If you don't have dried porcini mushrooms or porcini mushroom powder, use a more flavorful mushroom like cremini or portabella. You can find Porcini Mushroom Powder and Porcini Mushroom Salt at the Spice House (thespicehouse.com).

- This recipe makes a fairly thick soup. For a thinner soup, add an additional cup of water or vegetable stock.

- You can also use store bought/pre-made vegetable stock.

- I've added bite size pieces of meat to make this an even *heartier* soup.

Meat
....

Easy
....

GLUTEN
FREE*

SOUP

SERVES
6-8

CHICKEN LEEK SOUP

Modes: Sauté/Brown | Manual High Pressure   **Pressure Release:** Natural Release | Manual Release

A variation of your traditional Chicken soup, this super-fast to make soup uses boneless chicken thighs and aromatic spices for a hearty addition to your Shabbos Meal. This is a great recipe for when you are short on time before Shabbos. It takes minutes to make thanks to ready-made chicken stock and is incredibly fragrant. I often add more chicken and carrots to the soup. You can add your favorite additional vegetables too.

INGREDIENTS:

- 1 tablespoon olive oil
- 1 pound boneless skinless chicken thighs, cut into bite-size pieces
- 4 cloves minced garlic
- 1 small onion, coarsely diced
- 2 large leeks, chopped
- ½ pound carrots, sliced
- 4 cups Chicken Stock (see page 43)
- 2 cups water
- 1 tablespoon dried parsley flakes
- 1 teaspoon cracked rosemary
- 1 tablespoon dried thyme flakes
- ¼–1 teaspoon salt, to taste
- ¼–½ teaspoon freshly ground black pepper, to taste

1 Set the EPC to sauté/brown mode. Heat the oil in the EPC pot. Add the chicken and garlic. Stir frequently, using a heat resistant spatula, until the chicken is browned and thoroughly cooked, about 10 minutes. Keep the pot on sauté/brown mode.

2 Remove the chicken from the EPC pot and place it in a medium sized bowl or pan. Set aside.

3 Add the onion, leeks and carrots to the EPC pot. Cook about 5 minutes, stirring often. Scrape the bottom of the EPC pot to unstick any pieces of onion or garlic.

4 Add the chicken stock, water, chicken, herbs, salt and freshy ground black pepper to the EPC pot.

5 Lock the lid and close the pressure valve. Cook for 20 minutes using manual high pressure mode.

6 Naturally release the pressure for 30 to 45 minutes, then manually release the pressure.

Prepare the leeks by cutting off the roots and the very base of the stalk. Trim off the dark green top and pull off the tough outer leaves. Slice them lengthwise down the middle and rinse out any grit under running water.

Meat
....
Easy
....
GLUTEN
FREE*

MARGO'S SMOKY RED LENTIL SOUP

SERVES
6–8

<u>**Modes:** Sauté/Brown | Manual High Pressure **Pressure Release:** Natural Release | Manual Release</u>

I met my dear friend Margo online in her Facebook group Kosher Me & Gluten Free. We found we had a lot in common and often traded recipes via the group. A while after we had met online, we corresponded in a private message. I asked Margo where she was from and found out she lives only 3 blocks away, right here in Chicago!!! We've become even better friends and recipe tasting buddies since then. This is the favorite Friday night soup of Margo's family.

INGREDIENTS:

For the Soup

2 tablespoons olive oil

3 large onions, diced

3 stalks celery, diced

3 carrots, diced

3 large cloves garlic, minced

2 marrow bones

2 smoked hot dogs, such as Romanian's beef sticks, sliced

1 pound red lentils, rinsed

2 bay leaves

1 tablespoon tomato paste

¼ teaspoon cayenne pepper

¼ teaspoon freshly ground black pepper

salt, to taste

8 cups water

For the Hot Dog Croutons

1 teaspoon canola or avocado oil

1 regular hot dog, diced

For the Soup

1 Set the EPC to sauté/brown mode. Add the oil, onions, celery, carrots and garlic to the EPC pot. Sauté for about 5 minutes, until the vegetables are soft and browned.

2 Add the marrow bones and smoked hot dogs. Sauté, stirring periodically, until the bones are browned on both sides.

3 Cancel the sauté/brown mode. Add the 8 cups of water. Scrape the bottom of the pan with a heat resistant spatula, making sure no browned bits are stuck to the bottom. Add the remaining soup ingredients.

4 Lock the lid and close the pressure valve. Cook for 40 minutes using manual high pressure mode.

5 When the soup is finished cooking, naturally release the pressure for 20 minutes then manually release the pressure.

For the Hot Dog Croutons

6 While the soup is cooking, fry the regular hot dog pieces in the teaspoon of oil in a small skillet until browned.

To Finish

7 Serve the soup hot with fried hot dog croutons sprinkled on top.

- Margo says for a thinner consistency, you can use 10 cups of water, but be sure to add an extra tablespoon of tomato paste and one additional bay leaf.

- Romanian Kosher Sausage is an iconic Chicago institution. You can now order Romanian Kosher sausages, hot dogs, salami and other Romanian delicacies online.

STUFFED CABBAGE BEEF SOUP

SERVES
6-8

Modes: Manual High Pressure   **Pressure Release:** Natural Release | Manual Release

After making the Stuffed Cabbage, I often ended up with pieces of cabbage that weren't "stuffed cabbage worthy". Last year I also ended up with way too much sauce. I had the idea to combine the two together for an excellent Stuffed Cabbage Beef Soup! By simply cutting up the cabbage remnants, adding the leftover sauce, cubed beef, vegetables, and a little water, I had a rich, delicious, hot soup that's perfect for my cold Sukkah guests! Don't worry, if you don't have any leftovers from making Stuffed Cabbage…you can still make this soup from scratch!!

INGREDIENTS:

For the Soup Base

- 1 (28-ounce) can crushed tomatoes
- 1 (29-ounce) can tomato sauce
- 1 cup light brown sugar
- ½ cup apricot preserves or duck/sweet & sour sauce
- 8 cups water
- ½ cup finely diced onion (1 small)
- 1½ cups raisins
- 1 pound baby carrots
- 4 large stalks celery, sliced lengthwise down the center then into 2-inch pieces
- 5 cups cabbage, sliced (you can use remaining cabbage from the Stuffed Cabbage (Page 30) recipe)
- 2 pounds beef, cut into 1-inch cubes (you can use up to 3 pounds of beef for a "meatier" soup)

To Finish

- ½ pound wide egg noodles, cooked according to package directions (optional) crusty rolls, for serving

For the Soup Base

1 Add the Soup Base ingredients to the EPC pot. Stir gently to combine.

2 Lock the lid and close the pressure valve.

3 Cook using manual high pressure mode for 45 minutes. Naturally release the pressure for 30 minutes, then manually release the pressure.

To Finish

Add the egg noodles to the soup and serve to your hungry guests with hearty, crusty rolls.

You can make this recipe gluten free by using any shape of gluten free noodles, or by leaving the noodles out completely.

Meat

Easy

GLUTEN FREE*

TRADITIONAL CHICKEN SOUP

SERVES 6-8

Modes: Manual High Pressure   **Pressure Release:** Natural Release | Manual Release

There are few things on this planet that are traditionally more Jewish than Chicken Soup. It immediately invokes images of your Bubbie saying to you "Mamaleh, here…have some Chicken Soup with Matzoh Balls. It's good for you". In our family, Traditional Chicken Soup always had vegetables in it. The turnip and parsnip add special flavor, along with the more traditional carrots and celery usually found in chicken soup. The only time our family has pure, clear, vegetable free chicken soup is during the meal right before Yom Kippur when we only want G-d to see us in our purest form. It's tradition.

INGREDIENTS:

8–12 cups Chicken Stock (see page 43)

1 pound carrots, thinly sliced

6 stalks celery, thinly sliced

1 parsnip, cut into ¼ inch cubes

1 turnip, cut into ¼ inch cubes

1 tablespoon chopped fresh dill

1 tablespoon chopped fresh parsley

Salt and freshly ground black pepper to taste

Matzoh balls (optional)

1 Place the Chicken Stock in the EPC pot.

2 Add the vegetables to the stock. You can add additional chicken meat (saved from the Chicken Stock bones) if you like.

3 Lock the lid and close the pressure valve. Cook for 30 minutes using manual high pressure mode.

4 Naturally release the pressure for 30 minutes, then manually release the pressure.

5 Taste the soup and add additional spices, salt and freshly ground black pepper according to your personal preference.

6 Serve bowls of piping hot soup with the cooked soup vegetables, or fluffy matzo balls.

- You can add more or less vegetables according to your family's preferences. For a sweeter soup add a large, peeled sweet potato cut into small ¼ inch chunks.

- Leeks can also give the soup good flavor. Wash the leeks thoroughly, then slice thinly and add to the soup. Use only the light green part of the leek.

- You can add the chicken meat taken off the bones used to make the stock.

VEGETABLEY VEGETABLE SOUP

SERVES 6-8

Modes: Manual High Pressure   **Pressure Release:** Natural Release | Manual Release

Packed with vegetables, this easy to make soup is a great addition to any meal. The sweet potatoes, parsnip and turnip add extra sweetness to this heartwarming soup. You can also add whatever vegetables you find at farmer's markets, on the "buy today" shelf of your produce store, or you can just add your favorite vegetables.

INGREDIENTS:

- 1 medium onion, cut into eighths
- 1 pound baby carrots
- 3 stalks celery, cut into 1-inch pieces
- 1 large sweet potato, cut into 1-inch chunks
- 2 large zucchinis, cut in half lengthwise, then into ½ inch slices
- 1 large turnip, cubed
- 1 large yellow squash, cut in half lengthwise, then into ½ inch slices
- 1 parsnip, quartered lengthwise, then sliced

6–8 cups water, or vegetable stock

⅛–¼ cup consommé mix (optional), omit if using vegetable stock

Salt and freshly ground black pepper to taste

Croutons, for serving (optional)

Cooked shell pasta, for serving (optional)

1 Combine all the ingredients in the EPC pot.

2 Lock the lid and close the pressure valve. Cook for 30 minutes using manual high pressure mode.

3 Naturally release the pressure for 20 minutes then manually release the pressure.

4 Serve with croutons or your favorite cooked shell pasta.

I use natural consommé mixes without msg or unhealthy additives for extra flavor.

SERVES
6-8

DRIED FRUIT SOUP

Modes: Manual High Pressure   **Pressure Release:** Natural Release | Manual Release

Made from healthy dried fruits then chilled, it's perfect for a summer meal when you prefer a cold, refreshing soup. This recipe is incredibly simple to make with just 4 ingredients, and if you have extra less-than-stellar-looking fresh fruit in your refrigerator (like those apples that no one will eat) you can peel and dice the fruit and toss it in too. This soup is also great for wintertime when it's hard to get good in season fresh fruit. You can also serve this soup hot!

INGREDIENTS:

8 cups water

24 ounce dried fruit assortment

2 (3-ounce) packages raspberry gelatin

1 tablespoon freshly squeezed lemon juice

Additional peeled and cut up fresh fruit, for serving (optional)

Whipped cream, for garnish (optional)

1 Place the water, dried fruit, gelatin and lemon juice in the EPC pot. Gently stir to combine.

2 Lock the lid and close the pressure valve.

3 Cook for 20 minutes using manual high pressure mode. Naturally release the pressure for 30 minutes, then manually release the pressure.

4 Allow the soup to cool, then refrigerate for at least four hours until completely chilled.

5 Serve topped with whipped cream and additional fresh fruit if desired.

- You can get creative using different blends of fruit in this soup. Choose your family's favorites!

- Don't forget to get seedless dried fruit.

- Keep in mind the more prunes you use the darker the soup will be.

poultry

BROWN SUGAR CHICKEN

SERVES 6-8

Modes: Sauté/Brown | Manual Low Pressure **Pressure Release:** Manual Release

People often wonder where my recipes come from. Some are from my very active imagination…what if I put this ingredient with that ingredient? Many are variations of recipes I get being a notorious grocery cart snoop. When in the store aisles or checkout line, I snoop in my fellow shopper's carts and ask what they are making with the contents of their carts. Invariably I get some awesome, unique recipes. The recipe for a slightly different variation of Brown Sugar Chicken was given to me by my friend Judy while standing in the produce aisle of our local Kosher grocery store, Hungarian Kosher. It was going to be a super hectic pre-Shabbos sprint to the finish, and this recipe was supposed to be incredibly easy and delicious. Judy was right! It is! Thanks Judy!!

INGREDIENTS:

For the Chicken

- 6 chicken leg quarters, cut into thighs and drumsticks
- 2 cups light brown sugar
- 2 cups ketchup
- 2 tablespoons canola oil

To Finish the Sauce

- ½ cup cold water
- 3 tablespoons corn or potato starch

ADDED WATER

- ¾ cup water

For the Chicken

1 Set the EPC to sauté/brown mode. Add the canola oil to the EPC pot and brown the chicken in batches. Set the browned chicken aside on a plate, baking sheet or a casserole dish.

2 In a medium bowl combine the ketchup and light brown sugar, whisking until smooth.

3 Pour the ¾ cup added water into the EPC pot. Using a heat resistant spatula scrape any remaining browned bits from the bottom of the EPC pot. Place a rack into the pot.

4 Return the chicken to the EPC pot. Pour the sauce over the chicken.

5 Lock the lid and close the pressure valve.

6 Cook for 30 minutes using manual low pressure mode, then manually release the pressure.

7 Remove only the chicken from the EPC pot and place on a serving platter.

To Finish the Sauce

8 In a measuring cup, whisk the starch with the cold water until completely blended, making a slurry.

9 Set the EPC to sauté/brown mode. While whisking constantly, slowly pour the starch mixture into the sauce. Stir with a heat resistant spatula until thickened. Pour over the chicken.

Meat

Easy

GLUTEN FREE*

CAJUN FRIED CHICKEN

SERVES 4

Modes: Sauté/Brown

Every year, just after Passover, the GFEs (Gluten Free Eaters) of the world stock up on the "Non-Gebroks" (i.e. wheat free) products that are drastically reduced for quick sale once the holiday is over. One of my absolute favorite products to stock for the upcoming year is Nathan's Gluten Free Cajun Panko crumbs. They are so good that when I make Cajun Fried Chicken during the year everyone simply raves about how good it is – and they would never even guess its gluten free!

INGREDIENTS:

For the Egg Mixture

½ teaspoon sea salt

1 teaspoon onion powder

1 teaspoon garlic powder

¼ teaspoon freshly ground black pepper
   dash crushed red pepper

2 tablespoons canola oil

1 cup liquid egg, or 4 large room temperature eggs, well blended
   Additional Cajun Seasoning (see below), optional

For the Chicken

18 chicken breast tenders, or 3 large bone-less, skinless chicken breasts, tenders removed, and each cutlet cut into 5 long strips. You will have 5 to 6 strips per cutlet including the removed tender.

½ cup potato or corn starch

3 cups Cajun panko crumbs (can be gluten free) *or* plain panko crumbs and 2 tablespoons Cajun Seasoning (store bought or made with recipe below)

½ cup canola or avacado oil, for frying
   Cool Ranch Spread, for serving (page 144)

Cajun Seasoning

(based upon the Chowhound Cajun Seasoning Recipe)

2 tablespoons paprika

1 teaspoon kosher salt

2 teaspoons black pepper

2 teaspoons white pepper

2 teaspoons garlic powder

1 teaspoon dried thyme

1 teaspoon cayenne pepper

For the Egg Mixture

1 In a medium bowl, combine the salt, onion powder, garlic powder, freshly ground black pepper, crushed red pepper and canola oil with the liquid egg.

2 If you do not have Cajun Panko crumbs you can combine 2 tablespoons of Cajun Seasoning (see recipe below) to the liquid egg.

For the Chicken

3 Place the potato/corn starch in a casserole or baking dish.

4 Place the Cajun panko crumbs in a casserole dish.

5 Completely cover a chicken strip/tender with potato starch. Dip the coated chicken in the egg, covering completely. Place the chicken on the crumbs and press the panko onto it. Turn the chicken strip over and press the Panko crumbs onto the second side. Repeat with the remaining chicken strips/tenders.

6 Set the EPC to sauté/brown mode, then add the ½ cup canola/avocado frying oil.

7 Working in batches, fry the chicken strips/tenders, until both sides are golden brown.

8 Serve the Cajun Fried Chicken with Cool Ranch Spread

For the Seasoning

Combine the ingredients. Store in an airtight container.

- If you aren't lucky enough to have the Nathan's Panko near you, don't panic! I've given you a recipe for Cajun Seasoning to add to your plain panko crumbs.

- If making this chicken gluten-free, use Nathan's Gluten Free Cajun Panko crumbs. They are really good.

- Tenders are the "smusher" pieces that are attached to the underside of the chicken breast. They make awesome chicken fingers/nuggets.

Meat
......
Easy
......
GLUTEN
FREE*

CRISPY PANKO FRIED CHICKEN

SERVES
4

Modes: Sauté/Brown

Most of the books and posts that I've read state that it's simply not possible to fry in an EPC. "Preposterous!" I say. I probably wouldn't deep fry a small turkey in my EPC (there are way more efficient methods to cook a whole turkey), but it's great for "pan frying" cutlets without a lot of mess.

INGREDIENTS:

For the Egg Mixture

1 cup liquid egg, or 4 large room temperature eggs, well blended

2 tablespoons canola oil

1 teaspoon onion powder

1 teaspoon garlic powder

½ teaspoon sea salt

¼ teaspoon freshly ground black pepper

dash crushed red pepper

For the Chicken

1 cup potato or corn starch

2 cups plain panko crumbs (can be gluten free), plus an additional cup if necessary

18 chicken breast tenders or 3 large boneless, skinless chicken breasts, each cut into 6 long strips

½ cup canola or avocado oil for frying

BBQ Sauce, for serving

Cool Ranch Spread, for serving (page 144)

For the Egg Mixture

1 Whisk together the egg, canola oil, onion powder, garlic powder, sea salt, freshly ground black pepper and crushed red pepper in a medium bowl.

For the Chicken

2 Place the potato/corn starch in a casserole/baking dish. Place the panko crumbs in an additional casserole/baking dish.

3 Completely cover a chicken strip/tender with starch. Dip the chicken in the egg mixture, coating completely. Place each chicken piece on the crumbs and press the panko onto it. Turn the chicken over and press the Panko crumbs onto the second side. Repeat with the remaining chicken strips/tenders.

4 Set the EPC to sauté/brown mode, then add the ½ cup canola/avocado oil for frying.

5 Working in batches, fry the chicken pieces, until both sides are golden brown.

6 Serve the Crispy Panko Chicken with Barbecue Sauce, or Cool Ranch Spread.

I season this recipe simply. Feel free to add your favorite spices for a different flavor.

Meat
·········
Easy
·········
GLUTEN
FREE*

CHICKEN WITH RICE AND YUKON GOLD POTATOES

SERVES
6-8

Modes: Manual High Pressure **Pressure Release:** Natural Release | Manual Release

This recipe is basically an entire meal in a single EPC pot. Ok…maybe not an entire meal, but pretty close. I especially love this recipe because all the flavors from all the layers blend together for an "Oh My Goodness I want to eat the entire pot" EPC experience.

INGREDIENTS:

- 2 cups chicken or vegetable stock
- 1 cup water
- 1 cup rice blend (like Trader Joe's Basmati Rice Medley) or brown basmati rice
- 2 teaspoons dried minced onion
- 1 teaspoon dried minced garlic
- 1 pound baby Yukon gold potatoes, halved
- 3 pounds chicken legs, cut into thighs and drumsticks
- 1½ teaspoons onion powder
- 1½ teaspoons garlic powder
- 1½ teaspoons paprika
- ½ teaspoon freshly ground black pepper
- ½ teaspoon salt

1 Place the rice blend directly in the EPC pot. Add the dried minced onion and garlic. Pour the stock and water over the rice. Stir to combine.

2 Place a rack/trivet on top of the rice. Evenly set the potatoes on top of the trivet.

3 Place a second trivet over the potatoes. Carefully stack the chicken pieces on top of the second rack.

4 Sprinkle the onion powder, garlic powder, paprika, freshly ground black pepper and salt over the chicken.

5 Lock the lid and close the pressure valve. Cook for 20 minutes using manual high pressure mode. Naturally release the pressure for 25 minutes, then manually release the pressure.

6 Place the chicken on a large serving platter surrounded by potatoes and rice. Serve hot.

- One of the trivets need to be wire or a denser weave silicone so that the potatoes are separated from the other ingredients.

- I season this recipe fairly simply. Feel free to add your favorite spices for a different flavor.

MOM'S CHICKEN CACCIATORE

SERVES 8-10

Modes: Sauté/Brown | Manual High Pressure   **Pressure Release:** Natural Release | Manual Release

Everyone has heartwarming foods that remind them of their childhood. One of my favorite chicken recipe memories is my Mom's Chicken Cacciatore. It was Mom's go-to recipe, was relatively straight forward to make, and always generated huge applause from the family. It had to cook for a while to infuse the sauce flavors into the chicken, resulting in a melt-in-your-mouth soft chicken with an awesome sauce. The EPC is the perfect way to cook Mom's Chicken Cacciatore, with the pressure helping to blend the flavors and creating the perfect well-done chicken texture.

INGREDIENTS:

- 1 tablespoon canola oil
- 1 large sweet onion (like Vidalia), cut in half and thinly sliced
- 2 cloves garlic, minced
- 1 pound white button mushrooms, sliced
- 2 cups flour (can be gluten free)
- 1 tablespoon onion powder
- 1 tablespoon garlic power
- 1½ teaspoons paprika
- ½ teaspoon freshly ground black pepper
- ½ teaspoon sea salt
- 2 small (3-pound) chickens, cut into eighths (skin removed – optional)
- 1 (16-ounce) can tomato sauce
- 1 (6-ounce) can tomato paste

ADDED WATER

- 1 cup

1. Set the EPC to sauté/brown mode. Add the canola oil, then the sliced onion and minced garlic.

2. Sauté until the onions are slightly caramelized, stirring occasionally with a heat resistant spatula.

3. Add the mushrooms and continue cooking until the mushrooms are soft.

4. Turn off the EPC.

5. Remove the vegetables from the EPC pot and place in a medium bowl. Set aside.

6. Place the flour in a large casserole dish. Add the onion powder, garlic powder, paprika, freshly ground black pepper and salt. Stir to blend.

7. Add the 1 cup of ADDED WATER to the EPC pot. Scrape the bottom of the pot with a heat resistant spatula to remove any additional browned bits that may be stuck to the bottom.

8. Place a rack in the EPC pot.

9. Dredge each piece of chicken in the flour until completely coated. Set the coated chicken on the rack in the EPC pot. Repeat with the remaining pieces, stacking them evenly.

10. Cover the chicken with the tomato sauce. Top with the mushrooms and onions.

11. Lock the lid and close the pressure valve. Cook using manual high pressure mode for 20 minutes. Naturally release the pressure for 15 minutes, then manually release the pressure.

12. Remove the chicken and rack from the EPC pot.

13. Stir the tomato paste into the remaining hot sauce until it is completely blended.

14. Serve the chicken hot, topped with sauce, mushrooms and onions.

POMEGRANATE SYRUP CHICKEN

SERVES
6–8

Modes: Sauté/Brown | Manual Low Pressure **Pressure Release:** Manual Release

One day, when I was at my local restaurant supply store, I was looking at the flavoring syrups used for mixing drinks. There it was…pomegranate syrup!! It wasn't the concentrated pomegranate syrup made from actual pomegranates – it was a large bottle of flavored syrup (not a pomegranate to be found in the syrup). Perfect! It was thick, sweet, and had a great (imitation) pomegranate flavor. I added that syrup to pure pomegranate juice, added some honey and a few other ingredients for a Pomegranate Chicken marinade. If you top the chicken with a few fresh pomegranate seeds you have a beautiful Rosh Hashana main dish!! You can even make this dish ahead. Warm the syrup separately, then spoon it over the chicken just before serving. Fabulous!!

INGREDIENTS:

Nonstick vegetable spray

For the Chicken Marinade

2 cups pomegranate syrup
   (such as Torani)

1 cup pure pomegranate juice
   (such as POM)

½ cup honey

1 clove garlic, finely minced

¼ teaspoon freshly ground black pepper

¼ teaspoon ground thyme

4 pound chicken legs (thigh and drum-stick), skin removed (it's healthier!)

For the Sauce

¾ cup pure cold pomegranate juice
   (such as POM)

2 tablespoons corn starch

   Fresh pomegranate seeds for garnish
   (optional)

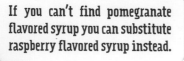

If you can't find pomegranate flavored syrup you can substitute raspberry flavored syrup instead.

Spray a 9-inch x 13-inch casserole with nonstick spray. Set aside.

For the Chicken Marinade

1 Combine the pomegranate syrup, pomegranate juice, honey, garlic, freshly ground black pepper, and thyme in a medium bowl. Stir until thoroughly combined.

2 Place the chicken bone side up in the prepared large casserole, or in a Jumbo Ziplock bag. Pour marinade over chicken.

3 Tightly cover the casserole dish with plastic wrap, or seal the bag and refrigerate the chicken for at least 2 hours.

To Cook the Chicken

4 Place a rack on the bottom of the EPC Pot. Add the chicken and the marinade.

5 Close the pressure valve then lock the lid. Cook using manual high pressure mode for 20 minutes, then manually release the pressure.

6 Remove only the chicken from the EPC pot and transfer to the prepared 9-inch x 13-inch casserole dish, leaving the marinade in the EPC pot. Remove the rack from the EPC pot.

For the Sauce

7 In a measuring cup or small bowl, whisk together the cold pomegranate juice and corn starch until thoroughly combined.

8 Set the EPC to sauté/brown mode.

9 Slowly whisk the pomegranate juice/starch into the remaining marinade. Stir constantly, using a heat resistant spatula, until the sauce thickens.

10 Spoon the sauce over the chicken.

11 Serve the Pomegranate Syrup Chicken sprinkled with fresh pomegranate seeds if desired.

Meat
....
Easy
....
GLUTEN
FREE*

RICE NOODLES WITH CHICKEN AND VEGETABLES

SERVES
6-8

Modes: Sauté/Brown | Manual High Pressure **Pressure Release:** Manual Release

In a large city like Chicago we are fortunate to have many charitable organizations that we can support. One of the groups that I belong to is AMIT. AMIT stands for "Americans for Israel and Torah, and is an American Jewish volunteer organization providing Jewish values–based education to 34,000 children in Israel. AMIT operates 106 schools and two surrogate family residences". It's a great organization and does a lot of great work in Israel. Our AMIT group organizes programs every year to raise money to send to the global AMIT office. One of the programs our group had was a cooking demonstration by the chef of Danzinger Kosher Catering. He showed us a recipe for "Pancit" a rice noodle and vegetable dish. It quickly became one of my family's favorites. I've modified the recipe for the EPC and changed a few ingredients but it's still a flavorful best-loved addition to our Shabbos meals.*

INGREDIENTS:

- 10 ounces medium width rice noodles
- 1 gallon boiling water
- ¼ cup toasted sesame oil
- 3 chicken breast halves, thinly sliced
- 1 teaspoon dried ginger
- 3 cloves garlic, finely chopped
- 4 cups thinly sliced green cabbage
- 6 ounces sliced shiitake mushrooms (around 4 cups)
- 2-3 large carrots, grated, or 10 ounces shredded carrots
- 1 cup chicken stock
- ¼ cup soy sauce (can be gluten free), or more to taste
- 6 green onions, sliced diagonally

1 In a large bowl, cover rice noodles with boiling water. Let the noodles soak for 15 minutes to 30 minutes until soft. Drain.

2 Set the EPC to sauté/brown mode. Add the toasted sesame oil, sliced chicken, ginger and garlic. Sauté, stirring constantly, until the chicken is browned.

3 Add the cabbage, shiitake mushrooms, carrots, stock, soy sauce, and rice noodles. Toss to coat.

4 Lock the lid and close the pressure valve.

5 Change the EPC mode to manual high pressure and cook for 8 minutes, then manually release the pressure.

6 Toss the drained rice noodles and green onions into the chicken and vegetables. Serve hot.

*https://en.wikipedia.org/wiki/AMIT

For a vegetarian option, you can substitute extra firm high protein tofu for the chicken or leave the chicken out completely.

SRIRACHA HONEY CHICKEN WRAPS

SERVES 6-8

Modes: Sauté/Brown | Manual High Pressure **Pressure Release:** Manual Release

The very first Memorial Day after Dear Son and Daughter-In-Law had gotten married, Dear Husband and I went to visit their new apartment and our exceptionally adorable Grandpuppy. The "kids" were excited to host and cook for us. We were super excited to be hosted and taste their cooking for the first time. Dear Son, found a "spicy" honey chicken recipe online that they prepared for Friday night. Holy Cow!!! The chicken was INCREDIBLY SPICY!! Nothing seemed to be able to relieve the heat enveloping our mouths and the steam coming out of our ears. After some discussion (and a lot of water) we realized that with a little less heat the Fantastically Spicy Chicken would make an excellent wrap when combined with cool Ranch Spread and healthy veggies. We had an amazing time visiting and got a terrific recipe as a bonus!!!

INGREDIENTS:

For the Sauce

¼ cup sriracha sauce

¼ cup honey

2 teaspoon soy sauce

1 teaspoon garlic powder

1 teaspoon dried minced onion

¼ teaspoon red chili flakes

For the Chicken

2 pounds chicken breasts, tenders removed

¼ cup sriracha sauce (see yellow note)

2 tablespoons canola or avocado oil

For the Wraps

1 large tomato, thinly sliced

8 ounces shredded lettuce, about 4-5 cups

3-4 large (10 to 12-inches) tortilla wraps

Jalapeño Cucumber Dip (see page 144)

Cool Ranch Spread (see page 144)

Guacamole, for serving

Salsa, for serving

Pareve sour cream, for serving

Decorative sandwich picks, for serving

ADDED WATER

½ cup water

For the Sauce

In a small bowl, combine the sauce ingredients. Set aside.

For the Chicken

1 In a medium bowl, coat the chicken breasts with the sriracha sauce (see yellow note on right).

2 Set the EPC pot to sauté/brown mode. When the EPC pot is heated add the canola/avocado oil.

3 Brown the chicken in batches on both sides, including the tenders. It helps to use a splatter shield to keep the oil from coating the kitchen.

4 Change the mode on the EPC to manual high pressure. Add the ½ cup ADDED WATER to the EPC pot and scrape the bottom to remove any stuck pieces of chicken.

5 Return the chicken to the EPC pot and cover with the prepared sauce.

6 Lock the lid and close the pressure valve. Change the mode on the EPC to manual high pressure mode. Cook for 10 minutes, then manually release the pressure.

7 Remove the chicken from the EPC pot and place in a 9-inch x 13-inch pan.

8 Using 2 forks, shred the chicken.

9 Add the remaining sauce from the EPC pot and toss to coat the shredded chicken.

For the Wraps

1 Place a tortilla on a flat surface. Spread the tortilla with a layer of Ranch Spread. Top with lettuce, tomato, and shredded chicken.

2 Tightly roll the tortilla around the filling. Secure with decorative picks.

3 Cut the wrap into 2-4 sections. You can serve with a decorative sandwich pick in each section.

4 Serve with additional Cool Ranch Spread, Jalapeño Cucumber Dip, guacamole, salsa, or pareve sour cream.

Before starting this recipe **TASTE YOUR SRIRACHA SAUCE!** Some sauces are stronger than others. When my friend Betty tried this recipe, she commented that her sauce was so strong that she didn't end up coating the chicken before browning it. She recommended adding this important note...if you have strong sriracha sauce, or prefer a milder wrap, add less sauce or completely skip the step #1 in the "For the **Chicken**" directions.

CAJUN CHICKEN WRAPS

SERVES
6-8

This recipe is similar to the Sriracha Honey Chicken Wrap recipe. It uses Cajun Fried Chicken which gives a spicy, crispy, crunchy filling contrasted with cool ranch spread and creamy avocado, making your taste buds dance the hora! You can also use leftover Cajun Chicken to make these wraps… if you somehow have a few pieces leftover.

INGREDIENTS:

4 large (10 to 12-inches) tortilla wraps
    Cool Ranch Spread (see page 144)

8 ounces shredded lettuce, about 4-5 cups

1 large tomato, thinly sliced

1 recipe Cajun Fried Chicken (see page 60)
    Decorative sandwich picks
    Jalapeño Cucumber Dip (see page 144), optional
    Guacamole, salsa, pareve sour cream, for serving

Modes: Sauté/Brown | Manual High Pressure
Pressure Release: Manual Release

1 Place a tortilla on a flat surface. Spread the tortilla with a layer of Cool Ranch Spread. Top with lettuce, tomato, and Cajun Fried Chicken.

2 Tightly roll the tortilla around the filling. Secure with decorative picks.

3 Cut the wrap into 2 to 4 sections (a decorative sandwich pick in each section).

4 Serve with additional Cool Ranch Spread, Jalapeño Cucumber Dip, guacamole, salsa, or pareve sour cream.

STRESS RELIEVING CHICKEN ROULADE

SERVES **6-8**

<u>**Modes:**</u> Sauté/Brown | Manual High Pressure <u>**Pressure Release:**</u> Manual Release

This chicken is incredibly good for you…it provides a constructive way to alleviate stress at the end of a busy, hectic and demanding day…by deliberately pounding the chicken (instead of your spouse!)!! I even sing an upbeat tune while whacking the chicken cutlets – it's great exercise and fun too! This chicken is also incredibly delicious with a covert layer of healthy, flavorful, natural smoked turkey breast, savory caramelized onions and vitamin packed spinach tucked into the roll. What could be better than coming into Shabbos stress and pressure free??

INGREDIENTS:

Nonstick vegetable spray

For Filling Option #1

- 1 tablespoon canola oil
- 1 small onion, finely chopped
- 2 cloves garlic, crushed
- 5 cups fresh baby spinach
- ½ cup panko crumbs
- 1 large egg

For Filling Option #2

- 1 tablespoon canola oil
- 4 large green onions, thinly sliced
- 1 clove garlic, crushed
- 1 pound shiitake mushrooms, sliced
- ½ cup panko crumbs (can be gluten free)
- 1 cup cooked brown rice
- 1 large egg
- Salt and freshly ground pepper to taste

For Filling Option #3

- 1 pound kishke, defrosted
- 1 large egg

For the Chicken

- 4 chicken breasts, tenders removed (around 2 pounds)
- ¾ pound natural smoked turkey breast, sliced

For the Sauce

- 1 cup apricot jam
- ¼ cup ketchup
- 1 tablespoon mustard
- 1 tablespoon soy sauce

ADDED WATER

- 1 cup water

ADDITIONAL ITEMS

- Mallet
- Heat proof, food safe plastic wrap or parchment paper
- 12 8-inch pieces of cooking twine

Line a large baking sheet with foil. Spray with non-stick vegetable spray. Set aside.

If Using Filling Option #1

1 Set the EPC to sauté/brown mode. Add the canola oil to the EPC pot.

2 Add the onion and garlic to the EPC pot and sauté until onions are slightly caramelized.

3 Add the spinach to the onion. Sauté until the spinach has completely wilted.

4 Turn off the EPC.

5 Add the panko crumbs and the egg to the spinach mixture. Stir until completely blended.

If Using Filling Option #2

1 Set the EPC to sauté/brown mode. Add the canola oil to the EPC pot.

2 Add the green onions and garlic to the EPC pot and sauté for one minute.

3 Add the mushrooms to the onions and garlic. Sauté until the mushrooms are soft.

4 Turn off the EPC.

5 Add the panko crumbs, rice and the egg to the mushroom mixture. Stir until completely blended.

If Using Filling Option #3

1 Blend the defrosted kishke with the egg until completely blended.

For all fillings

1 Divide the filling into 4 portions.

2 Tear a large sheet of plastic wrap, around 12-inches long.

3 Place a chicken breast on the plastic, and cover with another sheet of plastic, also around 12-inches long.

4 Pound the chicken with the mallet! Try to keep the thickness of the chicken even and pound it into as close to a square/rectangular shape as possible. Remove the top plastic sheet, leaving the chicken breast on the bottom plastic.

5 Place a layer of natural smoked turkey breast on the pounded chicken, leaving around 1½ inches uncovered on the far long end of the chicken.

6 Spread ¼ of the filling of your choice over the chicken.

7 Roll the chicken tightly around the filling towards the empty 1½ inch section.

→

8　Tie each chicken roll with 3 pieces of cooking twine. One piece on each end of the roll and one in the center.

9　Wrap a long piece of plastic tightly around the chicken roll. Twist the ends of the plastic to seal. Cover with a second long piece of plastic. Set aside.

10　Repeat with the remaining chicken breasts.

11　Place a rack/trivet on the bottom of a clean EPC pot. Add the 1 cup of ADDED WATER to the bottom of the EPC pot.

12　Carefully stack the rolled chickens on the trivet. Lock the lid and close the pressure valve.

13　Cook using manual high pressure mode for 20 minutes, then manually release the pressure.

14　Remove the chicken rolls from the EPC pot and place on a cutting board. Carefully unwrap the plastic from each chicken roll. Place on the prepared baking sheet.

15　Combine the sauce ingredients in a medium bowl. Spoon the sauce over the chicken rolls.

16　Broil the chicken rolls in the center of the oven for 10 to 15 minutes using medium heat until the sauce is bubbling and slightly caramelized on the top of the rolls.

17　Remove the chicken from the oven and let it rest for 10 minutes.

18　Remove cooking twine and slice the rolls into 1½ inch disks. Serve with warm pan sauce spooned over the chicken.

Meat

Easy

GLUTEN FREE*

SUCCULENT TURKEY BREAST ROAST

SERVES 6-8

Modes: Sauté/Brown | Low Pressure   **Pressure Release:** Natural Release | Manual Release

Here in hometown Chicago we are extremely fortunate to have multiple options for our Kosher meat. As a result, we never get bored because of limited selections, there's always something new to try! One of the healthier roasts I've found is the Turkey Breast Roast. It's shaped like a beef or veal roast in a mesh bag. The white turkey breast is way lower in fat and calories but still high in healthy protein.

INGREDIENTS:

4–4½ pound Turkey Breast Roast in a Mesh Bag

   No Bird Needed Stuffing (Page 96), optional

For the Sauce

1 cup sweet and sour duck sauce

1 (6-ounce) can tomato paste

1 tablespoon canola oil

1 teaspoon granulated onion

⅛ teaspoon marjoram

⅛ teaspoon white pepper

ADDITIONAL WATER

1 cup water

1 Mix the sauce ingredients in a medium bowl until smooth.

2 Place a rack in the bottom of the EPC pot, then add the 1 cup ADDITIONAL WATER.

3 Place the Turkey Breast Roast on the rack. Spoon the sauce over the turkey, completely covering the roast.

4 Lock the lid and close the pressure valve.

5 Cook for 55 minutes using manual high pressure mode. Naturally release the pressure for 15 minutes, then manually release the pressure.

6 Allow the roast to cool for at least 30 minutes before slicing.

7 Serve sliced turkey with pan juices and No Bird Needed Stuffing.

If you have trouble finding a Turkey Breast Roast, you can substitute a Chicken Roast or Veal Roast in a mesh bag. The mesh bag is important because it keeps the roast meat together while cooking.

Coca Cola Roast

Fresh Tomato Roast

Luscious Beauty Roast

Sweet and Sour Corned Beef

Cholent

Yapchik

Mom's Super Outstanding Veal Goulash

SERVES 6-8

COCA COLA ROAST

Modes: Manual High Pressure   **Pressure Release:** Natural Release | Manual Release

This is one of my all-time most interesting and favorite recipes. Yes, it's really made with Coke. Truly. What's cool about the cola is that the carbonation tenderizes the meat while it's cooking, and the cola taste is particularly excellent. The recipe is super-fast to make with only a few easily accessible ingredients, it's made with vegetables (healthy!), and you can have a cold drink of cola while preparing this yummy roast!

INGREDIENTS:

3–3½ pound beef roast

2 cups Coca Cola

⅔ cup orange juice

1 pound baby carrots

3 stalks celery, sliced lengthwise and cut into 3" pieces (or more if you like)

⅔ cup ketchup

¼ cup onion soup mix

1 Place a rack/trivet into the EPC pot. Place the roast on top of the rack.

2 Pour the Coca Cola and orange juice over the roast.

3 Carefully arrange the vegetables around the roast.

4 Pour the ketchup over the roast and vegetables, then sprinkle the onion soup mix over the roast/vegetables.

5 Lock the lid and close the pressure valve. Cook for 55 minutes using manual high pressure mode.

6 Naturally release the pressure for 30 minutes, then manually release the pressure.

7 Remove the roast. Wait 10 minutes, then thinly slice the roast. Place the slices in a roasting pan or casserole. Top with the vegetables and pan juices. Serve hot or cold.

- The easiest way to cut a roast is to place it in the refrigerator, preferably overnight, then slice the roast while its very cold.

- I use natural consommé and onion soup mixes without msg or unhealthy additives for extra flavor.

- You can substitute 1/4 cup of dried onion, or 1 large sliced onion, plus 1 teaspoon salt for the onion soup mix.

FRESH TOMATO ROAST

SERVES
6-8

Modes: Manual High Pressure **Pressure Release:** Natural Release | Manual Release

I always seem to buy too many tomatoes. I don't know if I have temporary memory lapse when I go to the store or am lulled into a hypnotic state by the rainbow of colored tomatoes, but I can't seem to stop buying them. Especially in the summer when there are even more heirloom varieties that have a rich tomato aroma wafting around them – even before they are cut. This roast recipe infuses the flavors of fresh, ripe tomatoes. MMMMMM.......

INGREDIENTS:

¾ cup vegetable or chicken stock

2½–3 pound beef roast (beauty roast, London broil)

1 (6-ounce) can tomato paste

2 tablespoons garlic infused oil (see tip below)

4 medium ripe tomatoes, diced

1½ cups thinly sliced onion or cippolini onions

4 cloves garlic minced

1 teaspoon sea salt

1 teaspoon onion powder

1 teaspoon garlic powder

½ teaspoon freshly ground black pepper

½ teaspoon crushed red pepper

1 Place a trivet/rack on the bottom of the EPC pot. Add the stock.

2 Completely cover the roast with the tomato paste (I wear gloves and just rub it onto the surface of the roast). Place the roast on the rack.

3 Place the garlic infused oil, tomatoes, onion, and garlic on top of the roast. Sprinkle the salt, onion powder, garlic powder, freshly ground black pepper and crushed red pepper on top.

4 Lock the lid and close the pressure valve. Cook using manual high pressure mode for 55 minutes. Naturally release the pressure for 30 minutes, then manually release the pressure.

5 Allow the roast to rest for at least 10 minutes before slicing. For best results, completely chill the roast in the refrigerator before slicing.

6 Top the sliced roast with the pan juices and vegetables.

• If you don't have garlic infused oil, substitute a mixture of 2 tablespoons olive oil and 2 cloves of freshly minced garlic.

• You can use more tomatoes if you like, just make sure they are ripe.

LUSCIOUS BEAUTY ROAST

SERVES 6–8

Modes: Manual High Pressure   **Pressure Release:** Natural Release | Manual Release

I admit that one of my least knowledgeable areas in the culinary world is beef. In my defense, when you have an awesome butcher who knows everything there is to know about meat, cuts of meat, and meat trivia, I find I can be a little lazier in my pursuit of meat expertise. If I ever find myself stranded on a deserted island with the only way to get off being meat knowledge, I'd be in trouble. Given the small chance of that happening, I'll rely on my hometown Chicago Romanian Kosher Sausage guys!

INGREDIENTS:

For the Roast Rub

- 1 tablespoon onion powder
- 1 tablespoon garlic powder
- 1 teaspoon paprika
- 1 teaspoon salt
- ½ teaspoon freshly ground black pepper
- ¼ teaspoon mustard powder
- ¼ teaspoon cumin

For the Roast

- 2½–3 pound beauty roast
- 1 (6-ounce) can tomato paste
- 1 large white onion, thinly sliced
- 1½ pounds small red potatoes, halved
- 1 pound baby carrots
- 1 pound sliced mushrooms

ADDED WATER

- 1 cup

For the Roast Rub

1 In a small bowl, combine the mustard powder, cumin, black pepper, onion powder, garlic powder, paprika and salt. Set aside.

For the Roast

2 Place a rack or trivet on the bottom of the EPC pot. Add the 1 cup ADDED WATER.

3 Rub the tomato paste all over the roast. Place the roast on the rack.

4 Sprinkle the Roast Rub over the roast.

5 Place the onion, potatoes, baby carrots and sliced mushrooms on top of the roast.

6 Lock the lid and close the pressure valve.

7 Set the EPC to manual high pressure mode and cook for 55 minutes.

8 Naturally release the pressure for 30 minutes, then manually release the pressure.

9 Remove the vegetables and roast from the EPC pot and place on a large cutting board or in a roasting pan.

10 Allow the roast to cool for at least 10 minutes, preferably 30, before slicing. For the easiest slicing, refrigerate the roast for at least 3 hours until completely cooled.

11 Top with pan juices and vegetables to serve.

- You can use up to a 3½ pound beauty roast or chuck roast for this recipe.

- You can also ask *your* favorite butcher for a recommendation.

SWEET AND SOUR CORNED BEEF

SERVES 6-8

Modes: Manual High Pressure **Pressure Release:** Natural Release | Manual Release

This recipe is great for when life is crazy and you're trying to get ready for Shabbos at the speed of light. Preparing it requires very little effort! To get melt-in-your mouth-tender, juicy, flavorful beef, EPC the meat for 30 min, then change the water and EPC again. You then make a simple glaze and bake it for a short time. It couldn't be easier. I once made the mistake of trying to roast a corned beef. UGH, it was one of the worst things I have ever made – it was like eating the Dead Sea. Cooking, draining, then re-cooking the Corned Beef helps to remove a significant amount of the salt – so simple…and so delicious!

INGREDIENTS:

For First Cooking

2½–3-pound corned beef brisket (deckle or pickled deckle)

Water to cover the beef

For Second Cooking

OPTION #1

1 cup water

OPTION #2

Water to cover the beef

Nonstick vegetable spray

For the Sauce

1 cup orange marmalade (or apricot jelly or duck sauce)

¼ cup Dijon mustard

¼ cup light brown sugar, packed

¼ cup ketchup

- **Corned beef will slice more easily if it has been refrigerated and completely cooled.**

- **You can cook the corned beef using Option #1 or Option #2. Option #1 will be delicious but slightly saltier than Option #2.**

For the First Cooking

1 Place the corned beef in the EPC pot. Cover with water without going over the max fill line.

2 Lock the lid and close the pressure valve.

3 Cook the beef for 30 minutes using manual high pressure mode.

4 Manually release the pressure, then unlock the lid.

5 Completely drain the salty water from the EPC pot.

For the Sauce

In a medium bowl, whisk together the marmalade, mustard, light brown sugar, and ketchup. Set aside.

For the Second Cooking

Place a shallow rack on the bottom of the empty EPC pot.

OPTION #1

1 Return the corned beef to the EPC pot. Cover with 1 cup of water.

2 Spoon the sauce over the beef.

3 Lock the lid and close the pressure valve. Cook for 30 minutes using manual high pressure mode.

4 Naturally release the pressure for 10 minutes, then manually release the pressure.

OPTION #2

1 Preheat oven to 350°F.

2 Return the corned beef to the EPC pot. Cover completely with water.

3 Lock the lid and close the pressure valve. Cook for 30 minutes using manual high pressure mode.

4 Naturally release the pressure for 10 minutes then manually release the pressure.

5 Spray a baking sheet with nonstick vegetable spray. Place the cooked corned beef on the baking sheet. Pour the prepared sauce over the beef.

6 Bake for 25-30 minutes until the sauce has thickened.

Allow the Sweet and Sour Corned Beef to cool for at least 10 minutes before slicing. Serve warm or cold, spooning the sauce over the beef.

Thanks Bayli Alter for holding the fork and knife!

CHOLENT

SERVES
6–8

Modes: Slow Cook Low Heat

I have heard from the grapevine that it can be difficult to make cholent in an EPC. Consensus is that cholent just comes out better in an old-fashioned slow cooker. After some thought, I concluded that one of the reasons is because of how the EPC cooks in comparison to a slow cooker. Most EPCs heat only from the bottom. A slow cooker's heat is generated on the bottom and up the sides, surrounding the inner pot with heat. It occurred to me that if you could simulate the surround heat, an EPC could cook a cholent as well as a traditional slow cooker does. By adding water around the outside of the inner cholent pan, you get the same (if not better) hot Shabbos cholent. It really does work!

INGREDIENTS:

ADDITIONAL MATERIALS

7-inch x 3-inch round pan with a tight-fitting lid

  Nonstick vegetable spray

½ cup barley or short grain brown rice (gluten free), divided

½ cup cholent bean mix, divided

2 large potatoes, peeled then cut into 3-inch pieces divided

1½ pounds cholent meat (I love Romanian Kosher's Cheek Meat)

1 pound kishke (can be gluten free), completely unwrapped

½ cup ketchup

  Onion soup mix, to taste (optional)

ADDED WATER

4 cups water or enough water to go ⅔ of the way up the outside of the 7-inch pan on the rack

1 Spray a 7-inch round pan and lid with non-stick vegetable spray.

2 Add ¼ cup barley/rice, ¼ cup cholent bean mix and half of the potatoes to the 7-inch pan.

3 Layer all the meat over the top of the barley/rice, beans, and potatoes.

4 Top the meat with the remaining potatoes, beans and barley/rice.

5 Place the unwrapped kishke on top the beans.

6 Tightly cover the 7-inch pan with the greased lid.

7 Place a rack/trivet with handles on the bottom of the EPC pot. Carefully place the round pan on top of the rack. Slowly pour the ADDED WATER around the pan. The water should come ⅔ of the way up the sealed pan.

8 Lock the lid and set the EPC mode to slow cook, temperature low heat, with the cook time setting to approximately 4 hours before you plan to use the Cholent (see tip).

9 When the EPC power is off, remove the Cholent from the EPC and serve hot.

- To make this cholent gluten free use gluten free short grain brown rice instead of barley and use gluten free kishke. I stock up on the gluten free kishke around Passover.

- Most EPCs will switch to warm mode for 4 hours after the cooking timer has expired. After those 4 hours the EPC will completely shut off. Please check with your user's manual to determine how your specific model of EPC works.

- You can find a 7-inch round pan on Amazon or in one of the well-stocked Kosher stores.

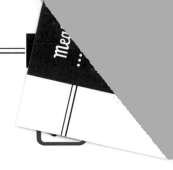
YAPCHIK

Modes: Slow Cook Low Heat

While it may have a bit of a funny name, the flavor of Yapchik is nothing to laugh at! It is similar to cholent in the fact that it cooks overnight and is eaten at lunch on Shabbos. Yapchik is more like a potato kugel with meat than a cholent like stew. When all the potato, onion and meat flavors are slow cooked together they produce an extremely rich delicious hot Shabbos dish!

INGREDIENTS:

ADDITIONAL MATERIALS

7-inch x 3-inch round pan with a tight-fitting lid

Nonstick vegetable spray

2 medium onions

4 large potatoes

⅓ cup potato starch

1½ teaspoons sea salt

1 teaspoon freshly ground black pepper

1 pound chuck or cheek meat

ADDED WATER

4 cups water or enough water to go ⅔ of the way up the outside of the 7-inch pan on the rack

1 Spray a 7-inch round pan and lid with non-stick vegetable spray. Set aside.

2 Using a food processor or box grater, alternately grate the onions and potatoes.

3 In a medium bowl, combine the grated onions and grated potatoes with the potato starch, sea salt and black pepper.

4 Spread half of the potato mixture into the prepared pan. Top with the meat, then spread the remaining potato mixture over the meat. Spray the top of the potato mixture with a heavy coating of non-stick spray

5 Cover the pan with the lid, or tightly cover with foil.

6 Place a rack/trivet with handles on the bottom of the EPC pot. Carefully place the round pan on top of the rack. Slowly pour water around the pan. The water should come ⅔ of the way up the pan.

7 Lock the lid of the EPC, then close pressure valve.

8 Set the mode to slow cook, temperature low heat, with the cook time setting to approximately 4 hours before you plan to use the Yapchik.

9 When the EPC power is off, remove the Yapchik from the EPC. Serve hot.

Most EPCs will warm for 4 hours after the cook time is over. After those 4 hours the EPC will completely shut off. Please check with your user's manual to determine how your specific model of EPC works.

MOM'S SUPER OUTSTANDING VEAL GOULASH

SERVES 6

Modes: Sauté/Brown | Manual High Pressure **Pressure Release:** Manual Release

Growing up, my mother had her "go to" recipes. She made an awesome tuna noodle casserole, meat sauce, and amazing Veal Goulash. When I was old enough to think about it, I asked my mother where she found her classic recipes. For a long time, she smiled and gave me the recipes but wouldn't tell me the origin. It was my Mom's thing. Later, she told me her secret. She had an old cookbook on the kitchen counter that she took a lot of the recipes from. She had modified them to make them her own, but the original recipes were in her blue cookbook. I knew that this cookbook was incredibly special to my mother and she would loathe to part with it. I went online to Amazon and was able to find the same version of my mother's book. While I know that she didn't want me to share the name (it's how she rolled) I did get permission to share her modified (then my modified) version of her veal goulash. Making it in an EPC makes the veal incredibly soft and tender, the best I've ever had. When I made it for my mother, I got a huge smile and an "It's really good!". I knew I had succeeded. The recipe I'm sharing with you is a prime example of taking a traditional recipe and making it traditional with a modern twist. Enjoy!

INGREDIENTS:

- 3 tablespoons canola oil
- 2 pounds veal for stew (veal in 1-1½ inch cubes)
- 1 cup celery, chopped
- 1 large onion, chopped
- 16 ounces tomato sauce
- ½ cup water
- 2 teaspoons granulated sugar
- 1 tablespoon paprika
- ¼ teaspoon freshly ground black pepper

For Finishing

- 6 ounces tomato paste
- 8 ounces wide egg noodles cooked
- 4 tablespoons freshly chopped parsley

  Additional paprika and parsley for garnish

1 Set the EPC to sauté/brown mode. Add the oil, then brown the veal in the oil.

2 Add the celery and onion and cook until the vegetables are tender.

3 In a small bowl, blend the tomato sauce, water, granulated sugar, paprika, and freshly ground black pepper. Pour over the meat.

4 Set the EPC to manual high pressure mode and cook for 25 minutes, then manually release the pressure.

For finishing

5 Stir in the tomato paste.

6 Toss the hot egg noodles with the freshly chopped parsley.

7 Serve Mom's Super Outstanding Veal Goulash over the noodles and garnish with additional paprika and parsley.

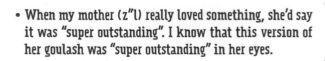

• When my mother (z"l) really loved something, she'd say it was "super outstanding". I know that this version of her goulash was "super outstanding" in her eyes.

Apple Pecan Squash with Goji Berries

No Bird Needed Stuffing

Beef Fry Fried Rice

Fruity Noodle Kugel

Greek Saffron and Baby Chickpea Rice

Saffron and Chickpea Rice for Dummies

Fragrant Pistachio Basmati Rice

Spaghetti Squash Yerushalmi Kugel

Honey and Rosemary Rainbow Carrots

Honeyed Carrots

Balsamic Beet Salad

side dishes & vegetables

Pareve

Easy

GLUTEN FREE*

APPLE PECAN SQUASH WITH GOJI BERRIES

SERVES 6

Modes: Manual High Pressure   **Pressure Release:** Manual Release

I first found goji berries in my favorite spice store, Rambam, in the Jerusalem market Machaneh Yehuda. They were different than any other berry I'd ever seen, and I really liked their flavor. I found that they are perfect in salads, rice, and other side dishes. Their red color really makes dishes pop. Don't forget to stop by Rambam and buy some of the "Sharon's Mix" and say hi to Chaim for me!

INGREDIENTS:

- 1 pound butternut squash, peeled, seeded and diced into ½-1 inch cubes
- 2 pounds (4 cups apples), peeled, diced into ½–1-inch cubes
- ½ cup light brown sugar or maple syrup
- 1 tablespoon olive oil
- 1 tablespoon freshly squeezed lime juice
- 1 teaspoon ground cinnamon
- ¼ teaspoon freshly grated nutmeg
- ¼ teaspoon salt
- ⅛ teaspoon freshly ground black pepper
- 1 cup chopped pecans
- 1 cup goji berries
- ½ cup dried cranberries

ADDED WATER

- 1 cup water

1 Place the cup of ADDED WATER into the EPC pot

2 Add the diced squash and apples.

3 Sprinkle the light brown sugar/maple syrup, olive oil, freshly squeezed lime juice, cinnamon, nutmeg, salt and freshly ground black pepper over the squash.

4 Lock the lid and close the pressure valve.

5 Cook using manual high pressure mode for 7 minutes, then manually release the pressure.

6 Stir the pecans, goji berries, and dried cranberries into the squash mixture. Serve warm.

If you have trouble finding goji berries substitute sweetened dried cranberries instead.

Pareve

Easy

GLUTEN FREE*

NO BIRD NEEDED STUFFING

SERVES 6-8

Modes: Sauté/Brown | Manual High Pressure   **Pressure Release:** Manual Release

When I found myself without ovens just before Rosh Hashanah my first reaction was to completely panic! Then I went to "Plan B". My ginormous raw turkey was not going to fit in my EPC, but my stuffing could! I had a lightbulb moment and "No Bird Needed Stuffing" was born. It was delicious, and Dear Brother-in-Law was remarkably impressed with the fact that I did not completely freak out (on the outside) given the circumstances! Hooray for me and my EPC!

INGREDIENTS:

ADDITIONAL MATERIALS

7-inch x 3-inch round pan with a tight-fitting lid

Nonstick vegetable spray

2 tablespoons canola oil

1 large onion, diced

1 cup carrots, diced

3 stalks celery, thinly sliced

1 pound mushrooms, sliced

10 ounces herbed croutons or 8 cups Corn Chex

1 large egg, lightly beaten

2 cups chicken or vegetable stock

ADDED WATER

1 cup

1   Spray a 7-inch x 3-inch round pan and lid with nonstick vegetable spray. Set aside.

2   Set the EPC to sauté/brown mode. Add the oil, onion, carrots and celery. Sauté until the vegetables are soft. Add the mushrooms and sauté until most of the liquid is absorbed. Turn off the EPC.

3   Stir in the croutons/Corn Chex, egg and chicken stock until completely combined. The stuffing should be moist and slightly squishy, but the croutons/Corn Chex should still be visible.

4   Transfer the stuffing to the prepared pan. Use a second pan if all the stuffing does not fit into one. You may need to run a second cycle if the stuffing doesn't fit into one pan.

5   Tightly cover the pan with foil or the lid. Place the pan on a rack with handles.

6   Rinse out the EPC pot, then return it to the EPC. Add the 1 cup of ADDED WATER to the EPC pot. Carefully lower the stuffing pan and rack into the EPC Pot.

7   Lock the lid and close the pressure valve. Set the EPC to cook for 15 minutes using manual high pressure mode, then manually release the pressure.

8   Serve hot with your favorite chicken or meat dish.

• Don't forget to make your makeshift aluminum foil handles (page 16) to lift the pan out of your EPC if you don't have a rack with attached handles.

• You can also easily double this recipe... just repeat the process with an additional pan. Super simple!!!

BEEF FRY FRIED RICE

SERVES
6-8

Modes: Sauté/Brown | Manual High Pressure   **Pressure Release:** Manual Release

Here's a little-known secret: You deli/butcher has something called "deli ends". These are the gold nuggets of the deli world. "Ends" are the best part of any salami, pastrami, corned beef, turkey roll, bologna, or roast beef. Deli ends are the ends of the deli that can't be sliced by the meat slicer, and generally pack the most seasoning, the most flavor, the best consistency and are the prize of the deli world. It's true. I often have to call my butcher in advance of coming and beg him to "SAVE THE ENDS!" for me. Invariably, if I don't call ahead, someone who got there just before me will take them all! Dear husband has banned deli ends from the house…. they are just too addictive! I still bring them in when I want to make Beef Fry Fried Rice – there is nothing better!

INGREDIENTS:

- 1 tablespoon olive oil
- 6-8 ounces Beef Fry, Facon (imitation bacon), or Deli Ends cut into ½ inch strips
- 2 large eggs, beaten
- 1 cup long grain brown rice (I like Uncle Ben's)
- 1 tablespoon soy sauce
- 1½ cups low sodium chicken or vegetable stock
- 8 ounces frozen mixed vegetables, thawed

1 Set the EPC to sauté/brown mode. Add the oil and fry the beef until crispy. Add the eggs and fry, stirring constantly, until scrambled.

2 Remove the beef and eggs from the EPC pot, and place in a large bowl or casserole dish.

3 Add the rice, soy sauce and stock to the EPC pot. Lock the lid and close the pressure valve.

4 Cook for 14 minutes using manual high pressure mode. Naturally release the pressure for 20 minutes then manually release the pressure.

5 Spoon the rice into the bowl/casserole with the beef and eggs. Add the thawed mixed vegetables and stir to combine. Serve hot.

You can use your favorite smoked meat for this recipe as well. Feel free to mix and match your favorite deli ends, even adding a little more…. because it's SO DELICIOUS!

FRUITY NOODLE KUGEL

SERVES
8

Modes: Manual High Pressure   **Pressure Release:** Natural Release | Manual Release

My husband calls Fruity Noodle Kugel "The ugly duckling of the Shabbos meal." I think when the kugel is as delicious and as pretty as this one, it should be called "The beautiful princess of the Shabbos meal". Anything that has fruit cocktail and maple syrup can't be anything but fabulous. I serve this kugel on a pedestal cake stand for dramatic effect because there is never enough drama at the Shabbos table.

INGREDIENTS:

ADDITIONAL MATERIALS

7-inch x 3-inch round pan with a tight-fitting lid

Nonstick vegetable spray

12 ounces wide egg noodles, uncooked

1 (29–30 ounce) can fruit mix with cherries in syrup

1 (20-ounce) can crushed pineapple, undrained

½ cup granulated sugar

¼ cup pure maple syrup

¼ cup canola oil

4 large eggs

¼ cup all-purpose flour

For Finishing

¼ cup light brown sugar

ADDED WATER

½ cup

1 Spray a 7-inch x 3-inch round pan and lid with nonstick vegetable spray. Set aside.

2 Mix the egg noodles, canned fruit (with the liquid), crushed pineapple (with the liquid), sugar, maple syrup, canola oil and large eggs together in a large bowl.

3 Fold in the flour.

4 Pour the mixture into the prepared pan. Cover with the tightly fitting lid.

5 Place a rack/trivet with handles on the bottom of the EPC pot. Add the ½ cup ADDED WATER to the bottom.

6 Carefully set the kugel on the rack. Lock the lid and close the pressure valve.

7 Set the EPC to high pressure mode and cook for 10 minutes using manual high pressure mode.

8 Naturally release the pressure for 30 minutes, then manually release the pressure.

9 Remove the kugel from the EPC pot and remove the kugel pan lid.

For Finishing

1 Sprinkle the top of the kugel with the ¼ cup brown sugar.

2 Place the kugel in the center of the oven and broil using medium heat for 5-7 minutes. The top of the kugel will turn a little brown and the sugar will become slightly bubbly.

3 Serve warm or cold.

Taking this kugel out of the pan can be a little tricky. When the kugel has cooled, run a knife around the edge of the kugel to loosen. Place a dinner plate on top of the kugel. Place one hand under the kugel pan and one hand on top of the dinner plate. In one fluid motion, flip the kugel onto the dinner plate. To get the kugel on the serving plate, repeat with a serving plate upside down on top of the inverted kugel.

GREEK RED SAFFRON AND BABY CHICKPEA BROWN RICE

SERVES 6-8

Modes: Manual High Pressure **Pressure Release:** Manual Release

Last year I went to the Fancy Food Show in New York. This show is HUGE, with food from all over the world. Nationalities are given different sections/rows of the show keeping culturally themed foods together. When I walked by the "Greece" section, I could actually smell the saffron coming from one of the booths' gorgeous display. I absolutely had to check out that saffron! I was given a small bottle and container as samples to try when I got back home. It was really the best saffron I have ever used.

Another Greek product I found was little baby chickpeas. So cute! They are supposed to be more flavorful due to the place and way they are grown. It was a no brainer to me to put the two together into a healthy, fragrant, and delicious new recipe. If you can't find these ingredients locally, don't worry. You can find them online or in a pinch, you can make the next recipe instead: Saffron and Chickpea Brown Rice for Dummies (see page 104).

INGREDIENTS:

- 1 cup Greek small chickpeas (see note)
- 2 cups short grain brown rice
- ½ teaspoon packed Greek saffron (see note)
- 1 tablespoon safflower threads (see note)
- 6 cups water
- 2 teaspoons sea salt
- ½ teaspoon freshly ground black pepper
- Pinch crushed red pepper
- 2 teaspoons canola oil

For Finishing

- 2 cups frozen chopped spinach (I like B'gan), defrosted and drained
- 2 green onions thinly sliced

1 Place the chickpeas, rice, saffron, safflower threads, water, salt, freshly ground black pepper, crushed red pepper and canola oil into the EPC pot. Lock the lid and close the pressure valve.

2 Cook for 35 minutes using manual high pressure mode.

3 Naturally release the pressure for 30 minutes then manually release the pressure.

For Finishing

4 Fluff the rice/chickpeas with a fork, then blend in the chopped spinach.

5 Fold in the green onions.

6 This dish is good cold or hot.

- If you can't find Greek Red Saffron, you can use regular saffron threads. Increase the amount of saffron to ¾ teaspoon.

- If you can't find small Greek chickpeas – substitute regular chickpeas.

- If you can't find safflower threads increase the saffron to ¾ teaspoon.

- Safflower threads can usually be found in the Mexican spice section of grocery and produce stores. They are sometimes listed as saffron but look more like flowers.

SAFFRON AND CHICKPEA BROWN RICE FOR DUMMIES

SERVES
6–8

Modes: Manual High Pressure   **Pressure Release:** Natural Release

When my dear friend Margo tested this recipe (thanks Margo!), she made it with long grain brown rice. She loved the rice and even said I should add a comment about how you could just make the rice and add other ingredients instead of the chickpeas and spinach. Now you know. I had an additional lively discussion with Margo about using the specialized ingredients in the previous recipe. In a moment of complete exasperation, I said "OK, I'll make another version and call it Saffron and Chickpea Brown Rice for Dummies" and so this way-simpler version of the recipe was born. I still think the earlier version is completely worth the effort, but this one is a most excellent substitute. Thanks Margo!

INGREDIENTS:

2 cups long grain brown rice

½ teaspoon packed saffron

1 tablespoon safflower threads (see note)

2 cups water

2 teaspoons sea salt

½ teaspoon freshly ground black pepper

   Pinch crushed red pepper

2 teaspoons canola oil

For Finishing

2 cups frozen chopped spinach, (I like B'gan), defrosted and drained

1 (15-ounce) can chickpeas, drained and rinsed (around 2 ½ cups cooked)

2 green onions thinly sliced

1 Place the rice, saffron, safflower, water, salt, freshly ground black pepper, crushed red pepper and canola oil into the EPC pot.

2 Cook for 20 minutes using manual high pressure mode. Naturally release the pressure for 30 minutes then manually release the pressure.

For Finishing

3 Fluff the rice with a fork, then fold in the spinach, chickpeas and green onions.

4 This dish is good cold or hot.

- Safflower threads can usually be found in the Mexican spice section of grocery and produce stores. They are sometimes listed as saffron but look more like flowers.

- If you can't find safflower threads increase the saffron to ¾ teaspoon.

- My friend Margo says that the saffron rice is so good you could eat it without the chickpeas and spinach!

Photo by Margo Strahlberg

FRAGRANT PISTACHIO BROWN BASMATI RICE

SERVES
6–8

Modes: Sauté/Brown | Manual High Pressure   **Pressure Release:** Manual Release

I'm a huge pistachio fan. They are crunchy and slightly sweet. When you eat them straight from the shell, they take forever to eat, which is a good thing if you want to limit the quantity of pistachios you eat. Years ago, I was trying to come up with something crunchy and sweet to add to my fragrant basmati rice. Given how much I love pistachios, they were an easy choice. I found that pistachios are often used in Middle Eastern and Persian cuisine along with cinnamon and raisins. Sautéing the cinnamon, onion, garlic and pistachios together, results in bringing out their rich, deep flavors.

INGREDIENTS:

3 cups brown basmati rice, rinsed until the water runs clear

1 cup water

3¾ cups vegetable stock

1 tablespoon olive oil

1 large onion, finely diced

1 clove garlic, minced

1½ cups pistachio nuts, shelled and salted

2 tablespoons onion soup mix

1½ teaspoons ground cinnamon, divided

1 cup raisins

½ teaspoon salt (optional if using a sodium free soup mix)

½ teaspoon freshly ground black pepper

Additional pistachios for garnish

1 Set the EPC pot to sauté/brown mode. Add the oil, onion and garlic. Sauté until the onions are slightly caramelized.

2 Add the pistachio nuts and ½ teaspoon of the cinnamon to the garlic and onions. Sauté for another few minutes until well combined. Remove the nut mixture from the EPC pot and place it in a large bowl or casserole dish. Do not clean the EPC pot.

3 Add the rice, water and vegetable stock to the EPC pot, then scrape the bottom with a heat resistant spatula to remove any stuck-on pieces.

4 Lock the lid and close the pressure valve. Cook for 20 minutes using manual high pressure mode. Naturally release the pressure for 10 minutes, then manually release the pressure.

5 Add the rice, remaining 1 teaspoon of the cinnamon, onion soup mix, raisins, salt, and freshly ground black pepper to the nut mixture. Mix until thoroughly combined.

6 Serve garnished with additional pistachios.

If you are politically opposed to using onion soup mix you can substitute 2 tablespoons dried onion instead of onion soup mix. Make sure to add the ½ teaspoon salt if omitting the mix.

SPAGHETTI SQUASH YERUSHALMI KUGEL

SERVES 6–8

Modes: Manual High Pressure | Sauté Mode   **Pressure Release:** Natural Release | Manual Release

I originally published this recipe on koshereveryday.com. At the time it was a revolutionary idea… using spaghetti squash for a kugel?!!! I've found that cooking the squash in the EPC is way faster/easier/better than the old baking method. It comes out perfectly! Here is what I wrote back in 2010: What can you make with squash… what can you make with noodles? You have made squash kugel with squash, you have made Yerushalmi kugel with noodles… put the two together and the concept of the Spaghetti Squash Yerushalmi Kugel is born. The squash really lends itself to the sweet and peppery kugel. The strands have a slightly sweet taste to them and hold up well when baked. When served, our Shabbos guests had to be told it's a squash kugel! They were extremely impressed with this radical and innovative new kugel. It was enjoyed by all – young and old. I guess when you have lemons you make lemonade – or the new adage… when you have spaghetti squash you make KUGEL!

INGREDIENTS:

ADDITIONAL MATERIALS

7-inch x 3-inch round pan with a tight-fitting lid

For the Squash

Nonstick vegetable spray

1 large spaghetti squash, cut in half lengthwise and seeded

ADDED SQUASH WATER

1 cup water

For the Caramel

1 cup granulated sugar

¼ cup water

¼ cup canola oil

1 tablespoon corn syrup

For the Kugel

4 large eggs

1 teaspoon salt

1 teaspoon freshly ground black pepper, (to taste)

ADDED KUGEL WATER

1 cup water

For the Squash

1 Place a trivet in the EPC pot. Add the squash and the 1 cup ADDED SQUASH WATER .

2 Lock the lid and close the pressure valve. Cook on high pressure for 7 minutes.

3 Manually release the pressure.

4 Remove the squash from the EPC pot and place in a large bowl. Scoop out the squash threads, discarding the peel.

5 Drain any extra liquid from the squash. Set aside.

For the Caramel

6 In a clean EPC pot, combine the sugar, water, oil and corn syrup. Stir to combine.

7 Set the EPC to sauté/brown mode. Cook stirring constantly until the granulated sugar is completely dissolved.

8 Continue cooking without stirring until the syrup is a deep amber color. Watch the syrup closely, it can burn.

9 When the caramel is done, quickly remove the EPC pot from the base.

For the Kugel

10 Pour the caramel/oil mixture over the warm squash. Stir until completely blended.

11 Add the eggs, salt and pepper and combine thoroughly.

COOKING METHOD #1: **TO COOK IN THE EPC:**

1 Spray a 7-inch round pan and lid with non-stick spray. Pour the Kugel Mixture into the prepared pan. Tightly cover with the lid.

2 Add the 1 cup ADDED KUGEL WATER to the EPC pot.

3 Place the pan on a trivet with handles. Carefully lower into the EPC pot.

4 Lock the lid and close the pressure valve.

5 Cook for 20 minutes on manual high pressure mode, then manually release the pressure.

6 Remove the pan from the EPC pot. Remove the lid from the pan, being careful not to get any water on the kugel.

COOKING METHOD #2: **TO BAKE IN THE OVEN:**

1 Preheat oven to 350°F or 325°F if using convection mode.

2 Spray a 9"x9" casserole dish with non-stick vegetable spray. Set aside.

3 Pour the kugel mixture into the prepared casserole dish. Place into the preheated oven and bake for 45 minutes, or until the top of the kugel is golden brown.

- It is important for the squash to be warm when pouring the caramel/ oil mixture over it. If the squash has cooled, place it in a microwave safe bowl and heat it for 5 minutes until completely warmed.

- You can use a 7-inch spring form pan to facilitate an easy removal of the kugel from the pan. Make sure your spring form pan fits into the EPC pot before using. Cover tightly with foil.

HONEY AND ROSEMARY RAINBOW CARROTS

SERVES
6-8

Modes: Manual High Pressure   Pressure Release: Manual Release

A few years ago, I found rainbow carrots in Trader Joe's right before Rosh Hashanah. I knew they would be a perfect and colorful addition to our holiday table. I've found colored carrots at other stores since and find that they are an easy and delicious way to brighten up any Shabbos or Holiday meal. The rosemary in this recipe gives a savory balance to the sweetness of the honey.

INGREDIENTS:

To Cook the Carrots

- 1 pound tri-colored carrots, scrubbed clean and cut into 2-inch pieces, or 1-pound baby rainbow carrots
- 1 tablespoon canola oil
- 1 tablespoon wildflower honey
- 1 teaspoon cracked rosemary, or 1 tablespoon chopped fresh rosemary

  salt and freshly ground pepper, to taste
- ½ cup vegetable stock

To Finish

- 3 tablespoons wildflower honey

To Cook the Carrots

1 Place the carrots in a large bowl and toss them with the oil, wildflower honey, rosemary, salt and pepper.

2 Place a steamer basket in the bottom of the EPC pot. Add ½ cup of vegetable stock to the EPC pot, then add the carrots.

3 Lock the lid and close the pressure valve. Cook for 6 minutes using manual high pressure mode.

4 Manually release the pressure. Remove the steamer basket from the EPC pot, leaving the carrots and sauce in the pot.

To Finish

5 Set the EPC pot to warm mode. Add the additional 3 tablespoons of wildflower honey to the carrots and toss to coat.

6 Allow the carrots to warm for an additional 10 minutes. Serve warm.

HONEYED CARROTS

INGREDIENTS:

- 1½–2 pounds multi-colored carrots, peeled, cut into 2-inch pieces
- ¾ cup honey
- 1 tablespoon canola oil
- ¾ cup water

Modes: Manual High Pressure
Pressure Release: Manual Release

1 Place all the ingredients in the EPC pot. Lock the lid and close the pressure valve.

2 Cook for 6 minutes using manual high pressure mode. Naturally release the pressure for 5 minutes, then manually release the pressure.

3 Transfer the carrots to a serving bowl and toss with the remaining liquid in from the EPC pot.

4 Serve warm or cold.

- If you can't find multi-colored carrots, you can use baby carrots or conventional carrots cut into 2-inch pieces.
- You can use different flavors of honey, like orange blossom honey, for new innovative versions of these recipes.

BALSAMIC BEET SALAD

SERVES
6-8

<u>**Modes:**</u> Manual High Pressure <u>**Pressure Release:**</u> Natural Release | Manual Release

It is a very very sad story. I am the only one in my entire family that will eat beets. It's true. Dear Husband will occasionally humor me and "taste" my beet creations with a "mmmmm…it tastes really…. beety….". Mind you, I would never make him eat a food that he completely detests, but it is a testament to how far he is willing to go to profess his profound love for me. Don't worry, I make sure to have his favorite Beef with Broccoli to make him happy and to profess my profound love for him!

INGREDIENTS:

2 tablespoons balsamic vinegar

¼ cup stevia or granulated sugar

1 tablespoon canola oil

⅛ teaspoon sea salt

Dash freshly ground black pepper

For the Beets

4 to 5 medium beets, scrubbed clean

ADDED WATER

1 cup

For the Dressing

1 In a small bowl combine the balsamic vinegar, stevia, canola oil, salt and freshly ground black pepper. Whisk until blended. Set aside.

For the Beets

2 Place a rack or steamer basket in the EPC pot. Add the 1 cup of ADDED WATER.

3 Place the beets in the EPC pot, then set the EPC pot on the rack.

4 Lock the lid and close the pressure valve. Cook for 10 minutes using manual high pressure mode.

5 Naturally release the pressure for 15 minutes, then manually release the pressure.

6 Drain the beets and transfer to a colander. Allow the beets to cool completely. The beets can be made a day in advance and stored covered in the fridge.

7 Rub the peels off the beets. The peels should come off easily after being cooled.

8 Cut the beets into ¼ inch thick strips. Place into a medium bowl.

9 Toss the beets with the prepared dressing. Serve immediately or refrigerate for up to two days.

- If you're lucky you can sometimes find different colored, multicolored, or striped beets in some produce stores. Each has a subtle different taste that gives this recipe lots of variations!

- I always wear disposable gloves when working with beets. Wearing disposable gloves also helps to grip the peel when rubbing the peel off cooked beets.

third meal

SEUDAS SHELISHIS

SUSAN'S PURPLE POTATO SALAD

SERVES 6–8

Modes: Manual High Pressure   Pressure Release: Manual Release

My dear Step-Mother-In-Law, Susan, is an awesome nutritionist. She is always suggesting healthy dishes and recipes that she has come across and developed. It's incredibly handy to have a family member who can answer all my diet and balanced nutrition questions. Susan is the one who suggested the original potato salad recipe "Lebanese Potato Salad". She knew I'd love it because it was a lighter potato salad recipe without mayonnaise. I've since updated the recipe to make it more fun and colorful, with purple potatoes, more corn, and sliced green onion. The colors of the salad potatoes and no heavy mayo make Susan's Purple Potato Salad beautiful, light, nutritious and delicious!

INGREDIENTS:

- 1–1½ pounds small purple potatoes, scrubbed
- 16 ounces fresh, canned or frozen corn (defrosted), drained
- ½ cup chopped fresh parsley
- 1 large green onion, thinly sliced
- 2 tablespoons extra-virgin olive oil
- ¼ cup freshly squeezed lemon juice
- ¾ teaspoon salt
- ¼ teaspoon garlic powder
- ⅛ teaspoon freshly ground black pepper

ADDED WATER

- 1 cup water

1 Place a rack in the EPC pot then add the 1 cup ADDED WATER. Place the potatoes in the EPC pot. Lock the lid and close the pressure valve.

2 Cook the potatoes for 4 minutes using manual high pressure mode. Manually release the pressure then transfer the potatoes to a colander to cool. You can refrigerate the potatoes for up to one day in advance before completing the next steps.

3 Cut the potatoes into quarters, then place in a large bowl.

4 Add the corn, parsley, green onion, olive oil, freshly squeezed lemon juice, salt, garlic powder and freshly ground black pepper. Carefully toss to combine.

5 This salad can be served immediately or refrigerated for up to one day. If the salad is not being served immediately, reserve the green onions and add to the salad just before serving.

If you can't find purple potatoes, you can use salad size red or Yukon gold ones instead.

SPICY EGGPLANT MATBUCHA

SERVES
6-8

Modes: Sauté/Brown | High Pressure   **Pressure Release:** Manual Release

Every Shabbos and Holiday we "collect" young professional adults who share our table and add life and energy to our lively meals. Somehow their numbers seem to grow during the week, and we are never completely sure how many guests we will have until the Shabbos meal starts. I often use our extended family as "guinea pigs", trying out new recipes and updated favorites. I made my first EPC pot of Spicy Eggplant Matbucha and served it at a lunch of our family plus 11 young adults. I set the Spicy Eggplant Matbucha on the table with the appetizers and the freshly cut challah, and waited for the assessment. I breathed a huge sigh of relief when it received rave reviews from the matbucha experts at the table! While I had made it slightly spicy the crowds concurred that it could be even spicier! If you are into flaming hot matbucha feel free to add additional crushed red pepper. Just remember, water spreads the heat…challah will help dissipate it!

INGREDIENTS:

- 1   medium sweet onion, finely chopped
- 1   clove garlic, minced
- 3   tablespoons extra-virgin olive oil
- 1   medium sized eggplant (around 1½ pounds), cut into half inch cubes
- 1   red bell pepper, diced
- 4   Roma tomatoes, diced
- 1   (6-ounce) can tomato paste
- ¼   teaspoon crushed red pepper or up to 1 teaspoon for super spicy Matbucha
- ½   teaspoon paprika
- ½   teaspoon salt
- ¼   teaspoon freshly ground black pepper

ADDED WATER

- ¾   cup water

1 Set the EPC to sauté/brown mode. Sauté the onion and garlic in the olive oil until soft. Add the ¾ cup ADDED WATER, eggplant, red pepper and tomatoes to the EPC pot.

2 Lock the lid and close the pressure valve. Cook on High pressure for 6 minutes using manual high pressure mode, then manually release the pressure.

3 Add the tomato paste, crushed red pepper, paprika, salt and freshly ground black pepper to the cooked eggplant. Stir to combine.

4 Chill before serving to meld all the flavors.

- The Matbucha may initially seem liquidy. It will thicken as it cools.
- This Spicy Eggplant Matbucha is also great on pasta and in omelets!

BLACKEST BLACK BEAN HUMMUS

SERVES 6-8

Modes: Manual High Pressure **Pressure Release:** Natural Release | Manual Release

Right after I made the Black Tahini (Page 145) I had to figure out what I could use it for besides the obvious…tahini. I polled my Facebook foodie friends and the consensus was to make black bean hummus using the Black Tahini. And so…a new recipe was born. Mazel Tov!

INGREDIENTS:

For the beans

2 cups raw black beans

2 cloves garlic

1½ teaspoon salt

  Water to cover beans by 2-inches

For the Hummus

2 tablespoons freshly squeezed lemon juice

2 tablespoons Black Tahini (Page 145)

1 teaspoon ground cumin

¼ teaspoon cayenne pepper

¼ teaspoon paprika

1 tablespoon extra-virgin olive oil

  Chips, crackers or pita, for serving

For the beans

1 Place the black beans and, garlic, salt and water in the EPC pot.

2 Lock the lid and close the pressure valve.

3 Cook for 30 minutes using manual high pressure mode. Naturally release the pressure for 20 minutes, then manually release the pressure.

4 Transfer the beans and garlic from the EPC pot to the bowl of a food processor, reserving the cooking liquid.

For the Hummus

5 Add the remaining ingredients and process until smooth, adding reserved cooking liquid to the hummus until the desired consistency is reached.

6 Serve with chips, crackers or pita.

If you don't have time to make the Black Tahini (although it's really good) you can use plain, boring traditional tahini to make this hummus.

SPEEDY TRADITIONAL HOMEMADE HUMMUS

SERVES 6–8

Modes: Manual High Pressure **Pressure Release:** Natural Release | Manual Release

Years ago, before hummus became a snacking staple, it was primarily a middle eastern dipping accompaniment. When I got my first EPC, I read everything I could to find out what pressure cookers excelled at cooking. I found out that the EPC cuts the cooking time of beans and chickpeas down to a fraction of the original cooking time. Woot! Speedy Traditional Homemade Hummus for everyone!

INGREDIENTS:

- 2 cups raw chickpeas
- 2 cloves garlic
- ½ teaspoon salt
- Water to cover chickpeas by 2-inches

1 Place the chickpeas, garlic, salt and water in the EPC pot.

2 Lock the lid and close the pressure valve.

3 Set the EPC to manual high pressure and cook for 30 minutes

4 Naturally release the pressure for 20 minutes, then manually release the pressure.

5 Transfer the chickpeas and garlic from the EPC pot to the bowl of a food processor, reserving the cooking liquid.

6 Add the remaining ingredients and process until smooth, adding reserved cooking liquid to the hummus until the desired consistency is reached.

- You can add different herbs and spices to this hummus to give it a different flavor.

- To make a spicy hummus add crushed red pepper, sriracha sauce, or schug to taste.

DAD'S EGG SALAD

SERVES
6-8

Modes: Manual Low Pressure   **Pressure Release: Manual Release**

While my father (z"l) may have been a very high-level executive at a major corporation, you could often find him repairing anything that needed fixing at our synagogue. You might have mistaken him for a maintenance man in his well-worn pants and flannel shirt, but he was a hands-on guy and took great pride in caring for what needed to be cared for, even if it meant getting his hands dirty. He was directly responsible for getting a homeland security grant to improve the security around the synagogue, he repaired the worn-out seats, replaced the stained-glass Mogen David on the front of the building and so much more. He also was an extremely gregarious and welcoming person. You could often find him in the shul kitchen making a breakfast of scrambled eggs for the men that had just finished early morning services. My father believed that if you could make it yourself you should, and that also applied to kiddush food. He often recruited me to partner in making kugels, cakes, sandwiches, soup, and other kiddush staples. He was famous for his egg salad recipe. Dad would add a little bit of pickle relish or "pickle Lilly" as he called it. It gave a little more color and flavor to the salad and everyone loved it when he made it. My father taught me the good deed of giving charity, but more importantly the lesson of immersing yourself in charitable acts.

INGREDIENTS:

To Cook the Eggs

6 large eggs

1 bowl ice water

To Make the Egg Salad

1 stalk celery, finely chopped (around ½ cup, can be chopped in a food processor)

2 large green onions, finely chopped (can be chopped in a food processor)

2 tablespoons mayonnaise

¼ teaspoon salt, or to taste

⅛ teaspoon freshly ground black pepper (or to taste)

1 tablespoon pickle relish (optional – although Dad would disagree)

ADDED WATER

1 cup water

To Cook the Eggs

1 Place the cup of ADDED WATER in the EPC pot. If you have an egg holder, place it in the EPC pot. If you don't have an egg holder use a standard EPC rack.

2 Place the eggs in the egg holder or carefully stack them on the rack.

3 Lock the lid and close the pressure valve.

4 Cook for 6 minutes using manual low pressure mode, then manually release the pressure.

5 Immediately transfer the eggs to the bowl of ice water to cool. Peel the cooled eggs and place in a large bowl.

To Make the Egg Salad

6 Mash the eggs by hand or using a food processor, pulsing until the eggs are chopped.

7 Stir in the celery, onions, mayonnaise, salt, freshly ground black pepper and relish (if using).

8 Serve with pita or crackers.

EDDIE'S TUNA SALAD

Eddie is a neighbor and dedicated member of our synagogue. You could frequently find him burning the midnight oil with my father, getting ready for a shul event or kiddush. Eddie's family and mine sponsor a "Simchas Beis Hashoeivah" event every year in memory of our loved ones that passed away. For many years the menu consisted of the Rebbetzin's split pea soup, tuna and egg salad sandwiches, salad, pasta and my homemade vegetable pasta sauce. The kids would have the time of their lives serving an ice cream extravaganza to the excited congregants, complete with all the toppings and whipped cream. One of Eddie's jobs was making a huge vat of tuna salad for the sandwiches. His secret ingredient (I have permission to reveal it) – Dad's Egg Salad. When added to the tuna it upgraded it to more than just a can of tuna with mayonnaise, it made a gourmet tuna salad. Thanks Eddie!

INGREDIENTS:

- 1 (15–16 ounce) can chunk light tuna in water, drained
- ¼ cup mayonnaise
- 1 green onion, chopped
- ½ cup Dad's Egg Salad (Page 122)

Place all the ingredients in a large bowl. Stir to combine.

In life it's important to have dear friends. If you are able, find friends like Eddie and his wife Anne. They are truly special, and we are blessed to count them as our family by choice.

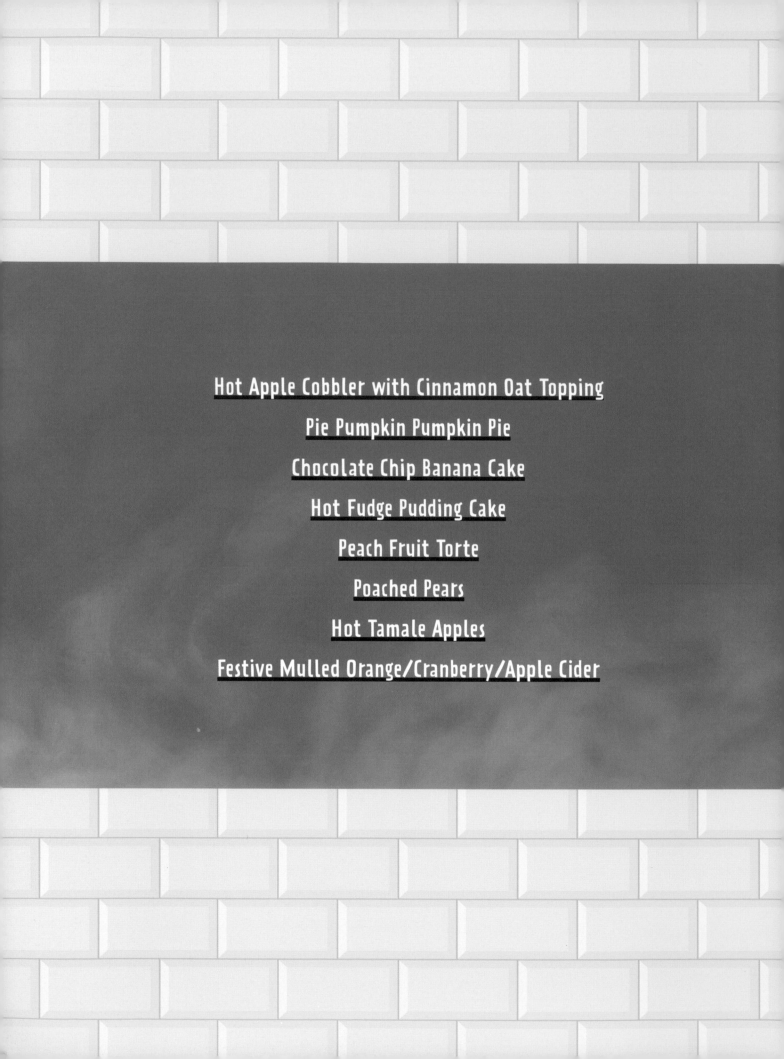

Hot Apple Cobbler with Cinnamon Oat Topping

Pie Pumpkin Pumpkin Pie

Chocolate Chip Banana Cake

Hot Fudge Pudding Cake

Peach Fruit Torte

Poached Pears

Hot Tamale Apples

Festive Mulled Orange/Cranberry/Apple Cider

HOT CRANBERRY APPLE COBBLER

SERVES
6-8

Modes: Manual High Pressure   Pressure Release: Manual Release

Nearly every year on Thanksgiving we have our friends, the Gutsteins, over for dinner. There are a lot of Gutstein's and that just makes the dinner a lot more fun! My dear fried Fran always asks what she can contribute to the meal and the answer is always the same, a dish that we have lovingly called "Franbler". Fran makes a special apple cobbler that is the best cobbler we have ever had. It is especially delicious warm, and if for some crazy reason it's not finished at the meal, you can find us sneaking leftovers out of the fridge, warming the bowl in the microwave and topping it with cold vanilla ice cream. YUM! While this isn't the exact recipe, Franbler is baked, I find this is a faster close cousin to the original. I strongly recommend having vanilla ice cream handy.

INGREDIENTS:

For the Cobbler:

Nonstick vegetable spray

8 cups peeled and sliced apples

12 ounces fresh cranberries

1 cup light brown sugar

½ cup granulated sugar

1 tablespoon cinnamon

⅛ teaspoon freshly grated nutmeg

2 tablespoons flour (can be gluten free)

3 tablespoons freshly squeezed lemon juice

1 cup water

For the Topping:

1 stick margarine (I use Earth's Balance)

1 cup rolled oats

¼ cup all-purpose flour

¼ cup light brown sugar

1 tablespoon ground cinnamon

⅛ teaspoon freshly grated nutmeg

For Serving

whipped cream (optional)

ice cream (optional)

For the Cobbler

1 Spray the EPC pot thoroughly with nonstick spray.

2 Place the apples, cranberries, light brown sugar, sugar, cinnamon, nutmeg, flour, freshly squeezed lemon juice and water into the EPC pot. Stir to combine.

3 Lock the lid and close the pressure valve.

4 Cook for 10 minutes using manual high pressure mode, then manually release the pressure.

5 Spray a 9-inch x 13-inch casserole dish with nonstick spray. Transfer the cobbler filling to the casserole.

For the Topping

6 In a medium bowl, using a fork, blend the topping ingredients. You want there to be "clumps". Sprinkle the topping over the filling in the casserole dish.

7 Place the pan under a low temperature broiler, around 10-inches from the heat source. Broil for 7- 10 minutes until the topping has browned.

For Serving

8 Serve the cobbler warm with whipping cream or ice cream.

Pareve
. . . .

Easy
. . . .

GLUTEN
FREE*

PIE PUMPKIN PUMPKIN PIE

SERVES
6-8

Modes: Manual High Pressure   **Pressure Release:** Manual Release

I subscribe to a surplus produce service called Imperfect Produce. Every week I go online and select imperfect (but very edible) or surplus produce and it gets delivered to my house every Monday. I get to be lazy (it comes right to my door!) and ecofriendly all at the same time. It's a win win situation. I love the feeling of doing something good for our planet and having the opportunity to get some very interesting produce. I've gotten my favorite pink lemons (yes, the inside is pink), purple radishes, multi colored beets, and even a pie pumpkin. What is the difference between a large jack-o-lantern pumpkin and a pie pumpkin? Carving pumpkins are larger, grainier, stringier and contain more water than the much smaller pie pumpkins. When you cook a real, honest to goodness pie pumpkin you get the perfect pumpkin filling for fragrant, festive, pumpkin pies! Way better than what you might get in a can. Make sure to get the pie pumpkins and not little ornamental pumpkins that are used to decorate for the holidays. While they may be tasty when fresh, you'd need an awful lot of them to make a pie! You can also find pie pumpkins at stores like Whole Foods and Trader Joe's, and if you're lucky some farmer's markets carry them in late fall.

INGREDIENTS:

- 1 small pie pumpkin, cut in half with seeds removed
- 1 (9-inch) deep dish pie crust, unbaked
- 3 large eggs
- ¾ cup granulated sugar
- ½ teaspoon salt
- 1 teaspoon ground cinnamon
- ¼ teaspoon ground cloves
- 1 cup pareve whipping cream or ¾ cup coconut cream
- Whipped topping for garnish

ADDED WATER

- 1 cup water

1 Preheat oven to 350°F.

2 Place a rack in the EPC pot. Add the 1 cup of ADDED WATER.

3 Add the pumpkin to the EPC pot. Lock the lid and close the pressure valve.

4 Cook for 15 minutes using manual high pressure mode, then manually release the pressure.

5 Remove the pumpkin from the EPC pot and place it in a large bowl. Allow it to cool completely.

6 Remove the pumpkin from the peel. Stir the pumpkin until it is completely smooth.

7 Add the remaining pie ingredients and whisk until smooth.

8 Pour the filling into the unbaked crust. Bake for 45-60 minutes until the crust is browned and the filling is set.

9 Refrigerate the pie for at least 1 hour.

10 Serve slices of pie with whipped topping.

To make this pie gluten free, use a gluten free pie crust. You can usually find them at Whole Foods in the gluten free frozen food section.

CHOCOLATE CHIP BANANA CAKE

SERVES
6-8

Modes: **Manual High Pressure**   **Pressure Release:** **Natural Release | Manual Release**

When I was growing up, my mother made the absolute best banana cake on the planet. The. Best. One of her secrets was finding extremely ripe bananas, the riper the better. You'd find us scoping out the rejected discounted produce rack for the best banana cake bananas. The banana cake and muffins were best right out of the oven. Warm and smushy. You could smell the banana essence wafting through the house on banana cake days. Mom's banana cake recipe is a prized possession and I still make it nearly every week. I'll share it with you. Shhh…. it's a secret family recipe. Ok, not so much anymore now that I've added and removed a few of the original ingredients. I've also changed some of the quantities to make it work for the EPC. Fine. It's not the same recipe at all anymore. Regardless, this recipe makes an excellent Chocolate Chip Banana Cake. You may need to make two. They have a tendency to magically disappear when hungry family is around.

INGREDIENTS:

   Nonstick vegetable spray with flour

4   tablespoons margarine

1   large egg

1   teaspoon pure vanilla extract

½   cup granulated sugar

3   medium/large ripe bananas

1   cup all-purpose flour, can be one-to-one gluten free flour

1   teaspoon baking soda

¼   cup orange juice

9   ounces chocolate chips

   Powdered sugar, for finishing

ADDED WATER

¾   cup water

• I have tried to make this recipe using muffin cups and mini bundt pans. It doesn't work well.

• If you don't have nonstick spray with flour, use a traditional nonstick spray.

---

1   Spray a 7x3 inch round pan with nonstick spray with flour. Set aside.

2   In a large mixing bowl of an electric mixer, cream the margarine, eggs, granulated sugar, and vanilla on medium speed.

3   Reduce the mixer speed and carefully add the ripe bananas, incorporating one piece at a time.

4   When the bananas are blended into the batter turn off the mixer, then add the flour and baking soda. Mix on slow speed, gradually pouring the orange juice into the batter.

5   Scrape down the sides of the bowl and continue to mix until the batter ingredients are completely blended.

6   Stir in the chocolate chips.

7   Pour the batter into the prepared round pan. Completely cover the pan with foil or a round lid.

8   Add the ¾ cup ADDED WATER to the EPC pot.

9   Place the cake pan on a rack with handles, or use a foil sling (page 16) around the cake pan. Carefully lower the cake pan into the EPC pot.

10   Lock the lid and close the pressure valve. Cook for 25 minutes using manual high pressure mode. Naturally release the pressure for 5 minutes, then manually release the pressure.

11   Remove the cake from the EPC pot, then carefully remove the foil from the cake pan being cautious not to get any moisture on the top of the cake.

12   In an EPC, the top of the cake will not brown. If you would like to have the top of the cake browned, place it in a pre-heated 350°F oven for 10 minutes.

13   Allow the cake to cool completely. Sprinkle powdered sugar on the cake.

14   Slice, then watch the cake disappear.

Pareve

Medium

GLUTEN FREE*

HOT FUDGE PUDDING CAKE

SERVES **6-8**

<u>Modes:</u> Manual High Pressure   <u>Pressure Release:</u> Natural Release | Manual Release

I have a fabulous cookbook collection, including many older books. Some of my absolute favorite cookbooks are the Hershey's Chocolate ones. They are almost always delicious, often creative, and always chocolate. How could that possibly be bad? When I first saw the original Hot Fudge Pudding Cake recipe in my favorite Hershey's Cookbook, I had to read it over around 50 times. Who pours water on the cake after it's in the pan???!!! I skeptically tried the recipe and it has been one of my family's favorites ever since. I've changed the recipe ingredients to make the cake less sweet and to accommodate the EPC cooking requirements. When the cake is done it will have a rich chocolate cakey bottom, a chocolate crust on top, and fudgy delicious chocolate pudding in the middle. No leftovers guaranteed!

INGREDIENTS:

For the Cake

Nonstick vegetable spray

1 cup flour (can be Gluten Free)

½ cup granulated sugar

½ cup pareve milk (soy, almond)

¼ cup canola oil

3 tablespoons cocoa powder

2 teaspoons vanilla extract

2 teaspoons baking powder

¼ teaspoon salt

For the Topping

½ cup packed light brown sugar

⅓ cup granulated sugar

¼ cup cocoa powder

1 cup hot water

For Finishing

Pareve vanilla ice cream (optional)

Whipped Cream (optional)

ADDED WATER

½ cup water

For the Cake

1 Spray a 7-inch x 3-inch pan with nonstick vegetable spray. Set aside.

2 In a medium bowl combine the cake ingredients. Blend until smooth. The batter will be thick.

3 Spread the cake batter in the prepared pan, evening out the top of the batter.

For the Topping

4 In a small bowl, combine the granulated sugar, light brown sugar, and cocoa powder . Evenly sprinkle the mixture over the batter in the pan.

5 Add the ½ cup of ADDED WATER to the EPC pot. Carefully place a cake pan on top of a rack with handles, then lower the rack into the EPC pot.

6 Carefully pour 1 cup of hot water *over* the cake topping *in the pan.*

7 Lock the lid and close the pressure valve.

8 Cook for 20 minutes using manual high pressure mode. Naturally release the pressure for 10 minutes, then manually release the pressure.

For Finishing

9 Serve warm in dessert bowls with pareve vanilla ice cream or whipped cream.

> **Note the highlighted instructions in the directions? Pay close attention to them. Each step is important and must be done correctly in order for the cake to have the creamy, chocolatey, pudding center.**

Pareve

Easy

GLUTEN FREE*

PEACH FRUIT TORTE

SERVES 6-8

<u>**Modes:** **Manual High Pressure**</u> <u>**Pressure Release:** **Natural Release | Manual Release**</u>

Dear Sister is a creative and accomplished culinary wizard in her own right. She also loves checking out the latest and greatest cookbooks and gadgets, and it's always fun when she is here and goes through my collections. Dear Sister lives in New Rochelle (yes, with Dick Van Dyke) and when she visits, she always brings a fabulous fun gift for me. Hooray! On one of her visits she brought the cookbook that the women from the Women's League Young Israel of New Rochelle put together "NEWvelle Rochelle." One of our favorite recipes from that book is the "Fruit Torte" by Rene and Gary Goldberg. Ironically, we have both adapted that recipe, and have added our personal touches to the original. Here is my version adapted for the EPC. I also used gluten free flour for our family but feel free to use the glutenous variety.

INGREDIENTS:

Nonstick vegetable spray

For the Peaches

4 peaches, cut into eighths (leave the peel on) or one-pound frozen sliced peaches, defrosted and drained

¼ cup granulated sugar

1 tablespoon freshly squeezed lemon juice

Dash freshly grated nutmeg

For the Cake

1 cup flour (can be gluten free)

¾ cup granulated sugar

½ cup melted margarine

2 large eggs

1 teaspoon baking powder

½ teaspoon grated lemon zest

Pinch salt

ADDED WATER

1 cup water

For the Topping

3 tablespoons light brown sugar

Nonstick vegetable spray

Pareve vanilla ice cream (optional)

Whipped cream (optional)

1 Grease a 7-inch x 3-inch round pan with nonstick vegetable spray. Set aside.

For the Peaches

2 In a medium bowl, toss the peaches with the ¼ cup sugar, freshly squeezed lemon juice and nutmeg. Set aside.

For the Cake

3 In a separate bowl, blend the ¾ cup sugar, margarine, eggs, salt, flour and baking powder.

4 Pour the batter into the prepared pan. Arrange the peaches in concentric circles around the top of the cake.

5 Tightly cover the top of the cake with aluminum foil.

6 Add the 1 cup ADDED WATER to the EPC pot. Carefully place a cake pan on top of a rack with handles, then lower the rack into the EPC pot.

7 Lock the lid and close the pressure valve. Cook for 40 minutes using manual high pressure mode, then manually release the pressure.

8 Remove the cake from the EPC pot, then carefully take the foil off the top.

For the Topping

9 Sprinkle the 3 tablespoons of light brown sugar over the top of the cake. Spray with nonstick vegetable spray.

10 Place the cake on the middle rack of the oven and broil using medium heat for 5 minutes until the sugar is melted and bubbly. Remove the cake from the oven and allow it to cool completely.

11 To serve, run a knife or offset spatula around the edge of the cake. Slice the cake into 6-8 slices. Serve with pareve vanilla ice cream or whipped cream.

Pareve

Medium

GLUTEN FREE*

HOT TAMALE BAKED APPLES

SERVES 8–10

Modes: Manual High Pressure   **Pressure Release:** Natural Release | Manual Release

My Mom (z"l) was a very creative cook. While she often made completely traditional dishes when the occasion warranted, she loved to be innovative when she could. I was the kid who always had a princess doll cake for my birthday parties, personally decorated by my mother. One of the delicious and original healthier desserts my mother made was baked apples with little red-hot candies. She would core out the seeds and stem from the apples and place those little round red cinnamon candies in the crevice. You know the candies…the ones that look like little bright red Advil pills. The candies gave a delicious cinnamon flavor to the apples, and we were always excited when she made them. Here is my updated EPC version of Mom's red-hot baked apples.

INGREDIENTS:

10–12 small Honeycrisp apples, cored from the top of the apple (try not to go all the way through the apple), around 3 pounds

48 Hot Tamale candies

2 cups sweet red wine

2 tablespoons brandy

1 cup packed light brown sugar

1 tablespoon cinnamon

¼ teaspoon freshly grated nutmeg

⅛ teaspoon ground ginger

Vanilla ice cream, for serving

1 Set a rack on the bottom of the EPC pot.

2 Place 3-4 Hot Tamale candies in the cored center of each apple. Carefully set the apples on top of the rack, placing a second layer of apples on the first if necessary.

3 Pour the wine and brandy over the apples. Sprinkle with the light brown sugar, cinnamon, nutmeg and ginger.

4 Lock the lid and close the pressure valve.

5 Cook for 5 minutes using manual high pressure mode. Naturally release the pressure for 5 minutes, then manually release the pressure. Carefully open the lid of the EPC pot. Using tongs, place the apples in a casserole dish. Pour the pan juice over the apples and then chill the apples (if desired).

6 Serve the apples with vanilla ice cream, topped with the pan juices.

These apples can be served hot or cold.

POACHED PEARS

Modes: Manual High Pressure   **Pressure Release:** Natural Release | Manual Release

You know how you find those cute little pears in the store and they are so adorable you have to buy them? Then you bring them home and you know you have to do something special with them because they were twice the price of the bigger traditional pears, simply because they are so small and cute. I fell into the "Oh, look how cute these little pears are!" trap a while back, just around the time I first got my EPC. I think you know where this is going…

INGREDIENTS:

10 small pears (around 3 pounds), cored and peeled

 1 (750-mL) bottle sweet red wine

½ cup honey

½ cup dried sweetened cranberries

¼ cup packed light brown sugar

 2 cinnamon sticks (around 3 inches each)

¼-½ teaspoon whole cloves

Pinch freshly grated nutmeg

Whipped cream or ice cream, for serving

1 Place a rack in the EPC pot. Place the pears in the EPC pot, standing with the stem side up.

2 Pour the wine over the pears. Add the cinnamon sticks, cloves, nutmeg, honey, light brown sugar and dried cranberries to the EPC pot. Lock the lid and close the pressure valve.

3 Cook for 8 minutes using manual high pressure mode, then manually release the pressure.

4 Transfer the pears to a deep casserole and pour the liquid from the EPC pot over the pears.

5 Serve the pears on a dollop of whipped cream, or with a scoop of vanilla ice cream. Ladle the pear sauce over the plated pears just before serving.

6 These can be served warm or cold.

I like to use ripe pears for this recipe. You could even buy the "use today" pears from the discount rack at your local produce store. Just use them right away!

Pareve

Easy

GLUTEN FREE*

FESTIVE MULLED ORANGE/ CRANBERRY/APPLE CIDER

SERVES 6-8

Modes: Manual High Pressure   **Pressure Release:** Natural Release | Manual Release

For our family, Thanksgiving is a super chill American Holiday that we celebrate by having a family dinner that always includes: Turkey, stuffing, roasted EPC potatoes, traditional green bean casserole, cranberry relish, creamy EPC sweet potato soup with candied pecans and whipped cream, and of course Pumpkin Pie (page 128). While Thanksgiving may be chill it's never boring. One year we had a string quartet from the Chicago Symphony Orchestra play before our meal. Other years we had a revolving door of dear friends with their 10 children rotating in for the meal. Super fun. My efforts to get the family to sing festive Thanksgiving songs are (rightfully) not met with tons of encouragement. At least I know that everyone will walk away full. It's a good Thanksgiving when Dear Husband points to me and announces "The Winner and Undefeated Champion", as I raise my clasped hands above my head in victory! If everyone loves the food and company, then we're all thankful winners!

INGREDIENTS:

64 ounces Apple Cider

3 cinnamon sticks

6 whole cloves

1 medium orange cut into 8 wedges

1 large apple cored and sliced

1 cup whole fresh cranberries

   Dash freshly grated nutmeg

¼ cup light brown sugar

1 Place all the ingredients in the EPC pot.

2 Lock the lid and close the pressure valve.

3 Cook 20 minutes using manual high pressure mode. Naturally release the pressure for 10 minutes, then manually release the pressure.

4 Serve in glass Irish Coffee Mugs during dessert or after the meal in front of a roaring fire.

You could make this drink a little more sophisticated by blending in a little of your favorite alcoholic beverage, like sparkling wine or rum.

Cool Ranch Spread

Cucumber Dill Sauce

Jalapeño Cucumber Dip

Spicy Sriracha Mayo

Black and White Tahini

sauces
& dressings

SAUCES & DRESSINGS

COOL RANCH SPREAD

SERVES 8

- ½ cup mayonnaise
- ½ cup pareve sour cream
- ¾ teaspoon dried dill weed
- ½ teaspoon dried parsley
- ½ teaspoon dried chives
- ¼ teaspoon onion powder
- ½ teaspoon garlic powder
- ¼ teaspoon fine sea salt
- ⅛ teaspoon finely cracked pepper

Blend all the ingredients in a medium bowl. Refrigerate for 30 minutes before serving.

Adapted from https://barefeetinthekitchen.com/homemade-ranch-salad-dressing/

SPICY SRIRACHA MAYO

- 1 cup mayonnaise
- 2 tablespoons sriracha sauce

Stir the mayonnaise and sriracha sauce together in a medium bowl until smooth. Refrigerate for at least 30 minutes.

Tip: Add more or less sriracha sauce depending on how spicy you'd like it.

CUCUMBER DILL SAUCE

SERVES 6–8

- 1 large cucumber, peeled and cut into 4-inch chunks
- ½ cup mayonnaise
- ½ tablespoon dried dill

Place the cucumber, mayonnaise, and dill in the bowl of a food processor fitted with an S blade. Pulse until smooth. Refrigerate for at least 1 hour before serving.

JALAPEÑO CUCUMBER DIP

SERVES 8

- 1 medium cucumber, peeled and cut into 4" chunks
- 1 large jalapeño pepper, cut in half and seeded
- 1 cup mayonnaise
- ¼ cup fresh cilantro
- Salt to taste

Place the cucumber, jalapeño pepper, mayonnaise and cilantro in the bowl of a food processor fitted with the "S" blade. Pulse until almost completely smooth.

Add salt to taste. Refrigerate for at least 1 hour before serving.

Pareve

Medium

GLUTEN FREE*

BLACK AND WHITE TAHINI

Modes: Sauté/Brown | Low Pressure   **Pressure Release:** Natural Release | Manual Release

SERVES
6-8

INGREDIENTS:

For Black Tahini

1 cup black sesame seeds

3 tablespoons canola oil

¼ teaspoon salt

For White Tahini

1 cup white sesame seeds

3 tablespoons canola oil

¼ teaspoon salt

1 Preheat a large skillet. Add the sesame seeds and cook over medium heat stirring constantly, 3-5 minutes. Be careful not to burn the seeds. You will know they are done when the seeds emit a nutty scent.

2 Allow the sesame seeds to cool completely.

3 Place the seeds in a food processor. Process them until they are smooth. Add the oil and salt and process until completely smooth.

Based upon the recipe from inspiredtaste.net

 **TOOLS & ACCESSORIES**

My Favorite Tools Brand Reference Sheet

Racks for the bottom of the Pot
Oxo Good Grips Silicone Pressure Cooker Rack
Turbokey Cooling Rack with Legs Diameter 7"

Racks with handles
Instant Pot Genuine Silicone Steam Rack
Instant Pot trivet with heat resistant silicon handles by Swift Stream
Oxo Good Grips Pressure Cooker Bakeware Sling

Steamer Baskets
Bastwe 6 quart Steamer Basket with Kitchen Tongs
Oxo Good Grips Stainless Steel Steamer with Extendable Handle
Sunsella Silicone Vegetable/Food Steamer Basket

Egg Cookers
2 pack Silicone Egg Bites Mold by Sunforest
Maxracy 2 piece Stackable Egg Steamer Basket Rack
Oxo Good Grips Silicone Pressure Cooker Egg Rack

Cholent/Yapchik Pot
CatchTheWave JACHNUN Aluminum Bowl Pot 16cm (6.2in)
iCloud Goods JACHNUN Aluminum Bowl Pot 18cm (7.09in)

7 inch Round Cake Pan
PME Round Seamless Professional Aluminum Baking Pan, 7"x4"

Non-Stick Pot and See Through Lid
Genuine Instant Pot Ceramic Non-Stick Interior Coated Inner Cooking Pot
Genuine Instant Pot Tempered Glass Lid

Additional Silicone Cooking Tools
StarPack Premium Silicone Kitchen Utensil Set (5 Piece)

Steam Vent Diverter
Steam Mates Henry – Steam Comes Out His Ears

Magnetic Cheat Sheet
BBTO Instant Pot Magnetic Cheat Sheet

Mini Silicone Pot Holders
Genuine Instant Pot Mini Mitts